Gondal's Queen

A Novel in Verse

AMS PRESS

NEW YORK

Portrait of Emily Jane Brontë by her brother, Patrick Branwell Brontë   *By courtesy of National Portrait Gallery, London*

Gondal's Queen

A Novel in Verse by Emily Jane Brontë

Arranged, with an Introduction and Notes
By FANNIE E. RATCHFORD

AUSTIN : 1955

UNIVERSITY OF TEXAS PRESS

Library of Congress Cataloging in Publication Data

Brontë, Emily Jane, 1818-1848.
    Gondal's queen.

    I. Ratchford, Fannie Elizabeth, 1888-   ed.
II. Title.
PR4172.G63   1973   821'.8   79-151965
ISBN 0-404-08929-1

Reprinted by special permission with the
University of Texas Press, Austin, Texas

Reprinted from the edition of 1955, Austin
First AMS edition published in 1973
Manufactured in the United States of America

AMS PRESS INC.
NEW YORK, N. Y.   10003

To my father and mother

Contents

Contents

Illustrations

Introduction

E MILY BRONTË'S poems were not written for publication or
for any eye save her own and, perhaps, her sister Anne's. By-
products of the long-continued Gondal Play and its secret prose
which she shared with her younger sister, they were unknown
even to other members of the Parsonage family until Charlotte,
in the autumn of 1845, accidentally stumbled upon one of her
sister's manuscript notebooks, precipitating a family crisis which
stands as a landmark in literary history.

Replete with weird names of unknown persons and places and
set down in minute, gnarled, and crabbed hand-printing, many
of them on mere scraps of paper, they tantalized and defied
would-be transcribers and editors for almost a century. The con-
sequent mutilated form in which they dribbled through to the
public, in small groups and single poems, served more, perhaps,
than all else to distort the world's understanding of Emily's
genius and to build up such familiar clichés as "the mysticism of
Emily Brontë" and "the mystery of *Wuthering Heights.*"

Now that C. W. Hatfield has brought the body of her verse to-
gether,[1] with text made perfect, it appears that the mutilation
was greater than had been guessed, that no one piece stands alone

---

[1] C. W. Hatfield, *The Complete Poems of Emily Jane Brontë*, Edited from
the Manuscripts (Columbia University Press, 1941).

but is part of a whole which in grandeur of conception and unity of meaning transcends the sublimest single poem. It is a tightly knit epic of the free, wild, grotesque world of imagination which nourished Emily's creative genius and brought it to glorious fruitage. It tells the story of genius at its strangest, and in view of the importance of its background I venture to repeat briefly the story told in *The Brontës' Web of Childhood*.[2]

On the night of June 5, 1826, the Reverend Patrick Brontë, perpetual curate of Haworth, in Yorkshire, returned from Leeds, bringing a toy each for his four children, who at that hour were in bed asleep. By request he had a box of wooden soldiers for Branwell, to replace an older set worn out by family play. Apparently the girls were more interested in the soldiers than in their own toys, and Branwell, next morning, when showing them his treasures, generously allowed each to choose a soldier for her own, to do with as she liked, though he remained the actual owner.

Around the twelve wooden soldiers, designated as the Young Men, the four Brontë children created through the days, weeks, months, and years a saga of group games called collectively the Young Men's Play, which they carried on with mounting gusto until Charlotte's departure for Miss Wooler's school at Roe Head in January, 1831. Details of its day-by-day development through these six years are recorded in Charlotte's and Branwell's diminutive play books, written and "published" under the names of certain of the wooden soldiers.

The play took permanent form when the children one day sent the Young Men, or the Twelves, as they often called the toys, "all true heroes," on a voyage in "the good ship Invincible—seventy-four guns," and allowed them to suffer shipwreck on the Guinea coast. The genii who haunted the "Gibble Kumri, or Mountains of the Moon"—the four young Brontës after reading *Arabian Nights* had assumed the roles of "Chief Genii" Talli, Branni, Emmi, and Anni, who ruled all subordinate spirits of land, water, and air—saved the party from the murderous blacks and built for them a magic city, which they called Glass Town or the Glass-

---

[2] Fannie E. Ratchford, *The Brontës' Web of Childhood* (Columbia University Press, 1941).

town,[3] at the mouth of the Niger River. As the play continued, the four chief heroes explored and conquered the surrounding country, each carving out a kingdom for himself. The four kingdoms became in course of time a confederation patterned after the United Kingdom of England, Scotland, Ireland, and Wales and dominated by the Duke of Wellington. The Glasstown Confederation, in its turn, became in course of further years and by Charlotte and Branwell's manipulation a far-flung Eastern despotism called Angria,[4] ruled by the elder son of the Duke of Wellington, young Arthur Wellesley, Marquis of Douro, who increased his power and added to his titles until at the height of his glory he signed himself "Arthur Augustus Adrian Wellesley, Duke of Zamorna and Emperor of Angria."

Because Emily's contributions to the literature of the Young Men's Play, i.e., her "books," if she wrote any, have been lost, her part in the creation must be inferred from a few passages in Charlotte's and Branwell's volumes. Charlotte records that Emily's own particular soldier was originally dubbed Waiting Boy, but later was given the more dignified and pretentious address of Sir William Edward Parry, after the great Arctic explorer. His kingdom in the Glasstown confederacy, known as Parrysland, stood in relation to Charlotte's and Branwell's countries as Scotland to England in the United Kingdom, its poverty, frugality and austerity contrasting with the commercial wealth, lavish luxury, and social brilliance of Charlotte's Wellingtonsland. The only direct description we have of Parrysland comes from Charlotte in person of Lord Charles Wellesley, younger son of the Duke of Wellington, reporting a recent visit to Parry's Palace for the October, 1830, issue of *The Young Men's Magazine*. Though Charlotte is here describing literally a group of toys (wooden figures, a toy village, etc.), she has Lord Charles emphasize, with

---

[3] I can find no reason to connect this name with the village on the Gaboon River, called Glass Town from its ruler, King Glass, described by Paul B. Du Chaillu in *Explorations and Adventures in Equatorial Africa*, published in London, 1861.

[4] Angria was the name of a family of pirates operating (1698–1756) from a fortified stronghold on the west coast of India. The young Brontës probably picked up the name in connection with Clive's 1756 defeat of Tulaja Angria.

a touch of contempt, the plainness of Emily's country in contrast to the *Arabian Nights'* richness and grandeur of her own Wellingtonsland.

In less than a week I crossed the borders & was immediately struck with the changed aspect of everything. . . . I saw none but little shiftless milk-and-water-beings in clean blue linen jackets & white aprons. all the houses were ranged in formal rows. they contained four rooms each with a little garden in front. No proud castle or splendid palace Towered insultingly over the cottages around No high-born noble claimed allegiance of his vassals, or surveyed his broad lands with hereditary pride. every-inch of ground was enclosed with stone walls. here & there a few regularly planted rows of trees generally Poplars appeared. But no hoary woods or nodding groves were suffered to intrude on the scene. rivers rushed not with Foam & thunder through meads & mountains, but glided canal-like along, walled on each side that no sportive child might therein find a watery grave Nasty factories with their tall black chimneys breathing thick colums of almost tangible smoke, discolored not that sky of dull hazy cerulean hue. every woman wore a brown stuff-gown with white cap & handkerchief Glossy satin, rich velvet, costly silk or soft muslin, broke not in on the fair uniformity.

Well "on I travelled many a mile" till I reached Parrys Palace. it was a square building of stone surmounted by blue slates and some round stone pumpkins the garden around it was of moderate dimensions laid out in round, oval or square flower beds, rows of peas, gooseberry bushes & black, red & white currant trees, some few common Flowering shrubs & a grass plat to dry clothes on. all the convenient offices such as, wash-house back-kitchen stable & coal house were built in a line & backed by a row of trees. in a paddock behind the house were Feeding one cow to give milk for the family & butter for the dairy & cheese for the table, one horse to draw the gig, carry—their majesties, or bring home provisions from market, together with a calf & foal as companions for both. . . . Sir Edward & lady Emily Parry came out to welcome their newly arrived guest. . . . Dinner was set on the table precisely at twelve o'clock. the dishes were roast beef, yorkshire pudding, mashed potatoes, Apple pie & preserved cucumbers. . . . At the dessert each drank a single glass of wine, not a drop more & eat a plateful of strawberries with a few sweet cakes. I expected some blow-up after the surfait [*sic*] which Ross if I might judge from his continued grunting & puffing had evidently got & was not disappointed. an hour subsequent to dinner, he was taken extremely sick. No Doctor being at hand Death was momentarily expected & would certainly have ensued, had not the Genius Emily arrived at a most opportune period when the disorder had reached its crisis. She cured with an incantation & vanished. I only remained at Parry's Palace till the morrow, for I found my visit intolerably dull as much so as I fear the reader will find this account of it[5]

It is apparent from a poem by Charlotte, coincident with her school days at Roe Head, that on the eve of her departure from the parsonage the four children, sitting as "Chief Genii in Council," decided to obliterate their creation in a grand spectacular finale:

> The Trumpet hath sounded, its voice is gone forth
> From the plains of the south to the seas of the north;
>
> . . . .
>
> 'Twas the Ruler of Spirits that sent forth the sound
> To call his dread legions in myriads around.
>
> . . . .
>
> Mute, mute are the mighty, and chilled is their breath,
> For at midnight passed o'er them the Angel of Death!
> The king and the peasant, the lord and the slave,
> Lie entombed in the depth of one wide solemn grave.

Branwell, however, did not accept the obliteration, but continued the Glasstown play at high speed with such co-operation as could be had from Charlotte through letters and vacation visits. Emily, refusing his leadership, took advantage of the interruption to withdraw and set up a play of her own with Anne, leaving her brother to struggle alone until Charlotte's return in midsummer, 1832. Eagerly Charlotte's hungry pen fell upon the old creation as a channel for a new romantic stream drawn from her reading of Byron and Scott.

Despite protest, voiced by Branwell in the *Glasstown Intelligencer*, Emily remained aloof with Anne, and from that time on, until Branwell sank out of the family life, the children played and wrote in pairs, Charlotte and Branwell, Emily and Anne, the two groups maintaining a parallelism of plot development which argues close knowledge each of the other's writings, and on

[5] Now in the Bonnell Collection, Brontë Museum, Haworth, England.

Emily's part a conscious and studied antithesis of philosophy and moral judgment, advanced, no doubt, in protest against fallacies of the earlier creation.

In my early study of the Brontë juvenilia, I had small interest in Emily, for of the "good many" books which she and Anne enumerate in their birthday notes of 1841 and 1845,[6] none have come to light. She first challenged my interest in a transcript of a hitherto unannounced journal fragment sent me by H. H. Bonnell, of Philadelphia, a singularly sincere and devoted Brontë collector, who through a number of years reassembled a large proportion of the scattered literary remains of the family. The fragment, in Emily's handwriting, dated November 24, 1834, and signed for herself and Anne, is a mere roll call of the parsonage household, with the whereabouts and occupations of each at the moment.

Taby said just now Come Anne pilloputate (i e pill a potato [ )] Aunt has come into the kitchen just now and said where are your feet Anne Anne answered On the floor Aunt papa opened the parlour door and gave Branwell a letter saying here Branwell read this and show it to your Aunt and Charlotte—The Gondals are discovering the interior of Geraldine [*sic*] Sally Mosley is washing in the back-kitchin.

Commonplace and embarrassingly childish it seemed to me for a girl well into her seventeenth year. But for one sentence I should have taken little notice of it. That one sentence, "The Gondals are discovering the interior of Geraldine," fastened itself in my brain and clung the tighter because it made no sense. The Gondals I knew from the birthday notes as the people of Emily and Anne's play world, but who (or what) was Geraldine and why the Gondals should be interested in her (or its) interior was beyond my guessing.

The question was still teasing my imagination when Hatfield's revision of Clement K. Shorter's *Complete Poems of Emily Jane Brontë*[7] came off press. I fell upon it eagerly, reading and rereading it until I had its poems by heart, their moods and emotions as

[6] See Appendix II.

[7] *The Complete Poems of Emily Jane Brontë*. Edited by Clement Shorter. Arranged and collated, with Bibliography and Notes by C. W. Hatfield (London, Hodder and Stoughton, 1923).

Earliest extant writing by Emily Jane Brontë, a journal fragment signed for herself and her sister Anne, containing the first reference we have to the Gondal-Gaaldine creation

First seven stanzas of poem that carries both internal Gondal date and date of composition, in Emily's hand-printing, from her manuscript notebook headed "Gondal Poems." (The initials A. B. N. are those of Charlotte's husband, Arthur Bell Nicholls, indicating that this is one of the poems he copied out while the manuscript was still in his possession. The Nicholls' copy is in the Huntington Library, San Marino, California.)

well as their words. The poems did not tell me why the Gondals were concerned with the interior of Geraldine, but, far better, they gave me an exciting glimpse of a mountainous lake-dotted land inhabited by an Ossian-like race who loved and hated passionately, warred mysteriously, and died heroically.

Correspondence with Mr. Hatfield advised me that the volume was incomplete and inaccurate in text. In editing it, he explained, he worked from transcripts sent him by Shorter;[8] to correct the errors which he discovered after its publication, he was now gathering photographic copies of Emily's scattered manuscripts in order to prepare independently a complete and perfect edition. He admitted the possibility of my suggestion that the poems, groups of them at least, were related to each other in an over-all story pattern,[9] but he was not concerning himself with that pattern; his task was to establish the text and date the poems.

The opportunity to follow up my awakened interest in Emily Brontë came with a Guggenheim Foundation award, 1929–30, for work in England. In the Bonnell Collection, recently transferred by terms of Mr. Bonnell's will to Haworth Parsonage, I found the original of the teasing journal fragment, and with relief I read, "The Gondals are discovering the interior of"—not Geraldine, but—"Gaaldine." The name was strange to me, but it carried a probable geographical connotation; "The Gondals are

---

[8] Patrick Brontë outlived all his children, dying in 1861. His heir was his son-in-law, A. B. Nicholls, to whom went the family possessions, including the literary remains of Charlotte, Emily, Anne, and Branwell. Mr. Nicholls returned to Ireland, where, in 1894, Shorter, acting for himself and T. J. Wise, sought him out and purchased from him the greater part of the Brontë papers. Except for a few items which he kept for himself, Wise fed the manuscripts into the market, keeping transcripts of those in which he or Shorter saw publication possibilities. It was from such transcripts that Shorter drew his long list of Brontë books.

[9] It was several years later that I came across an article entitled "Gondaliland," by Madeleine Hope Dodds (*Modern Language Review,* January, 1923, 9–21), which attempted to fit a group of Emily Brontë's poems into a Gondal story plot. Insufficient and erroneous data led Miss Dodds into errors, but hers was the first published attempt, so far as I know, to identify Emily's poems with her play world. Miss Dodds followed this article with "A Second Visit to Gondaliand," October, 1926. She took her titles from Shorter's misreading of Emily's birthday note of 1841, "Gondaliand" for "Gondalians."

discovering the interior of Gaaldine" made sense. I had not too long to wait before Anne Brontë satisfied in part my mounting curiosity.

In the same collection I found *A Grammar of General Geography for the Use of Schools and Young Persons*, by the Rev. J. Goldsmith, London, 1823, still warm from use by the four young Brontës. Into "A vocabulary of proper names ... to be committed to memory," Anne had penciled:

ALEXANDIA [*sic*], a kingdom in Gaaldine.
ALMEDORE, a kingdom in Gaaldine.
ELSERADEN, a kingdom in Gaaldine.
GAALDINE, a large island newly discovered in the South Pacific.
GONDAL, a large island in the North Pacific.
REGINA, the capital of Gondal.
ULA, a kingdom in Gaaldine, governed by 4 Sovereigns.
ZELONA, a kingdom in Gaaldine [written Zalona by Emily].
ZEDORA, a large Provence [*sic*] in Gaaldine, Governed by a Viceroy.

Here, to my intense excitement, was an outline map of Emily's Gondal-Gaaldine world. To it I fitted, as best I could, the geographical and personal names found in the poems as I now knew them, for I had already studied Emily's manuscripts[10] in the Brontë Museum, made rich by the recent Bonnell bequest, and had collated the Ashley Library notebook with the Shorter-Hatfield text. I had also had a look at the manuscript volume which is in the library of Sir Alfred J. Law at Honresfeld, in Lancashire, and which I knew of from Davidson Cook's analysis of it.[11] Gondal, I saw, was an island set in a stormy sea, in winter a land of

> ... mists and moorlands drear,
> And sleet and frozen gloom,

with "twilight noons and evenings dark."[12] It was a mountainous

---

[10] For a full description of all known Emily Brontë manuscript poems, see Hatfield, *The Complete Poems of Emily Jane Brontë* (1941), pp. 24–26.

[11] "Emily Brontë's Poems," *The Nineteenth Century and After*, August, 1926, 248–262.

[12] Peculiarly enough, Emily gave to her cold, rugged North Pacific kingdom the name of a tropical Indian state, Gondal in the peninsula of Kathiawar.

country crossed by streams and dotted with lakes, the most familiar being Lake Elderno and Lake Elmor (also written Elnor) surrounded by Elmor Moors and Elmor Scars. In summer it was a sparkling land, green with fern and ling, bright with flowers, and gay with swallows and larks. Politically it was divided into four or more kingdoms or principalities—Gondal, Angora, Alcona, and Exina, and possibly others not mentioned in the poems. Its capital was Regina on Lake Elderno, a city of great buildings, including the national cathedral—"twice the summer's sun has gilt Regina's towers," I read in one of Anne's poems.

Gaaldine in the South Pacific was in main a tropical country. Ula, or Ulah, "a kingdom in Gaaldine governed by 4 sovereigns," was characterized by

> Her tropic prairies bright with flowers
> And rivers wandering free,

matching her "Eden sky." "Zedora's strand" was shadowed by "palm-trees and cedars towering high." Zalona's tragic day of defeat dawned "all blue and bright in golden light." Of the other divisions of Gaaldine—Alexandria, Elseraden, and Almedore—I could learn nothing, except that Julius Brenzaida of Angora was also King of Almedore.

Back in Austin, Texas, I had in my hands for a time a group of thirty-three additional poems (later bought by W. T. H. Howe and now in the Henry W. and Albert A. Berg Collection, New York Public Library) in tiny hand-printing, on twenty leaves of various shapes and sizes. A few months later two other poems on small bits of paper came into the Stark Library at the University of Texas. In 1936 came the climax of the long search, when I learned that a manuscript volume of Emily's verse, which in private hands had been refused both Mr. Hatfield and myself, had come into the British Museum. I soon had a photostat copy before me. As its heading, "Emily Jane Brontë. Transcribed February, 1844./GONDAL POEMS,"[13] indicated, it proved the most

[13] This volume was not included in the Shorter-Wise purchase of Brontë family manuscripts from A. B. Nicholls in 1894. It, with other Brontë treasures retained by Nicholls, was sold at Sotheby's on July 26, 1907. The purchaser was Mrs. George Murray Smith, widow of Charlotte's pub-

important, from my point of view, of the several groups I had seen. Thanks to Emily's own occasional headings of the individual poems, which up to this time had been omitted for the most part from the printed editions, my early guess, long since strengthened into conviction, was now a demonstrable certainty: many, perhaps all, of her poems, including those most exploited by theorizing biographers as subjective, were actually units in a flaming epic of a purely imaginary world and its people.

My card file, as nearly complete as I could make it, showed four distinct groups of poems centering around outstanding characters, the largest group being that held together by a woman designated as A. G. A. One poem, signed "A. G. Almeda," revealed her surname—never repeated—and the text of two others supplied Augusta; the middle initial, G., remained an unknown for several years longer. The A. G. A. group, in its turn, was broken into smaller groups concerned with (1) Alexander, Lord of Elbë, (2) Lord Alfred S. of Aspin Castle, (3) Fernando De Samara, and (4) Lord Eldred W. Another main group had for its common factor Julius Brenzaida, whom I gradually identified under other designations: King Julius, Emperor Julius, Julius of Angora, Almedore, J. B., and J. A. This, too, had subgroups, one dominated by Emperor Julius's queen, variously called Rosina, Rosina of Alcona, Rosina Alcona, and Alcona, and another connecting him with a woman called Geraldine, who in one poem elopes with him and in another speaks as the mother of his child. Closely connected with both of the Julius groups, yet distinct enough to stand as a unit, were poems pertaining to his political and territorial rivals, the royal families of Exina and Gleneden, probably one and the same, Gleneden being the family name, Exina its territorial title. Weaving through all was a dark boy of sorrow whose full name and identity never come clear.

I found it helpful also to group these same poems and all others according to subject, mood, tone, and emotion, under such head-

---

lisher. From her son it came into the British Museum. At the same time (February, 1844) that Emily arranged this manuscript volume, she set up a second notebook, without title (referred to on p. 18 as in the library of Sir Alfred Law, of Honresfeld, in Lancashire), in which none of the entries has an identifying heading.

ings as ambition, war, conquest, defeat, imprisonment, loyalty, treason, foreboding, grief, and remorse.

The problem now was the relation of the several groups to each other.

Unhappily there was no day-by-day prose record of the development of Gondal to guide me, such as I found for Glasstown and Angria in Charlotte's and Branwell's juvenilia. I recognized, however, certain Gondal grotesqueries as survivals from the early family play shared by the four children. The college dungeons and the Palace of Instruction, for instance, were understandable in light of Charlotte's "Tales of the Islanders" (March 12, 1829– July 30, 1830):[14]

In June, 1828, we erected a school on a fictitious island, the Island of Dream, which was to contain one thousand children. The island was fifty miles in circumference, and certainly appeared more like the work of enchantment and beautiful fiction than sober reality. . . .

In the hall of the fountain, behind a statue, is a small door over which is drawn a curtain of white silk. This door when opened discovers a small apartment, at the further end of which is a very large iron door to a long dark passage. At the end is a flight of steps leading to a dark subterranean dungeon. . . .

At the end of this dungeon are the cells which are appropriated to the private and particular use of naughty children. These cells are darkly vaulted and so far down in the earth that the loudest shriek could not be heard by any inhabitant of the upper world. In these, as well as in the dungeon, the most unjust torturing might go on without any fear of detection, if it were not that I keep the key of the dungeon and Emily keeps the key of the cells and of the high iron entrance which will brave any assault except with the lawful instrument.

The children who inhabit this magnificent palace are composed only of the young nobles of the land.

The Palace of Instruction was further explained by passages in Charlotte's "The Foundling," written May 31–June 27, 1833,[15] which at the same time suggest the nature of the Unique Society.

[14] In the Berg Collection, New York Public Library. Quotations are taken from *Cosmopolitan Magazine* for October, 1911, 611–622.
[15] In the Ashley Library, British Museum.

Gondal's Queen

At a distance of nearly six hundred miles from the continent of Africa there lies an island called the Philosophers' Island. . . . Embosomed in . . . a valley . . . the only building on the Island stands . . . a sort of college or university for the instruction of the rising generation. Here the most learned philosophers of the world have their residences, and to this place all the noble youths of Verdopolis are sent for their education. There has lately been formed among the professors and tutors of the University a secret society of which many of the principal characters in our city are members. This association is said to have dived deeply into the mysteries of nature and to have revealed many of her hidden and unthought of secrets.

Emily and Anne's birthday exchanges made certain two facts of fundamental importance. First, an extensive prose literature of Gondal had once existed, and a few of its titles—"A History of the First Wars," "Gondal Chronicles," "Augustus Almeda's Life," and "The Emperor Julius's Life"—identified it as the background of the Gondal poems. Second, the chronology of Gondal followed closely that of Angria, its "First Wars" corresponding to the conquest of the Glasstown country by the original wooden soldiers; the discovery and conquest of Gaaldine, to the expansion of Glasstown into Angria; King Julius's wars of aggression by which he made himself Emperor of the Gondal-Gaaldine world, to young Arthur Wellesley's rise to the dignity and power of "Arthur Augustus Adrian Wellesley, Duke of Zamorna and Emperor of Angria"; and its civil war between Royalists and Republicans, to the Republican uprising in Angria led by Percy, Earl of Northangerland, against Arthur Wellesley.

Gradually other parallels to Angria appeared, often amounting to antitheses of moral viewpoint. Angria's emperor, young Arthur Wellesley, was an arch-Byronic hero, for love of whom noble ladies went into romantic decline and commoners gave their lives with nun-like devotion; Gondal's queen was of such compelling beauty and charm as to bring all men to her feet, and of such selfish cruelty as to bring tragedy to all who loved her— death in battle to Alexander, banishment and suicide to Lord Alfred, madness and suicide to Fernando. It was as if Emily was saying to Charlotte, "You think the man is the dominant factor in romantic love; I'll show you it is the woman." From Angria's stirring patriotism, Emily stripped the veil, to show ruthless aggression with its attendant miseries; and in place of Charlotte and Branwell's pageantry of war—marching soldiers, waving banners, and martial music—Emily showed wounded and bleeding men, devastated countrysides, and broken homes. To Emily war was real and terrible.

I had, then, to guide me, first of all, a background of familiarity with the Young Men's Play which Emily had shared and from which Gondal took its fundamental structure; Charlotte and Branwell's Angria, which it paralleled; and, in addition, Anne's companion Gondal poems, not nearly so many in number as Emily's and markedly inferior in epic spirit, yet offering valuable leads and in several cases directly confirming or contradicting my guesses.

I had evidence, too, that, notwithstanding the growing and perhaps shifting nature of the Gondal creation, Emily was working out an over-all design comparable to the clear-cut blueprint of *Wuthering Heights*. Four of her poems, for instance, carry in their headings, along with dates of composition, internal plot dates indicating a well-established Gondal chronology, such as "From a Dungeon Wall in the Southern College. J. B. [Julius Brenzaida], 1825"; "From a D—— W—— in the N.C. A.G.A. Sept., 1826"; and "Written on Returning to the P. of I. on the 10th of January, 1827." And I found in the Brontë Museum, Haworth, a scrap of paper on which Emily had listed a number of Gondalan characters, with height, age, and coloring of each. I conclude, therefore, that Gondal was a compact and well-integrated whole, rather than the sprawling, formless thing some would make it.

Most obvious of all, and the surest positive guides in reconstructing the Gondal story from the poems, were Emily's own headings. On the negative side, however, these very headings offered serious difficulties; in several cases they were even misleading, for Emily, anticipating modern alphabetism, reduced most of her personal names to initials. Delighting, even as Charlotte and Branwell, in multiple designations for her various characters, she used interchangeably, and without explanation, letters standing for any one of the individual's several Christian names, his family name, and his multiple titles—as well as end-

less combinations of them all. Worse still, sets of initials fitted
equally well several known characters in the Gondalan drama, to
say nothing of possible unknowns. "A. S.," for instance, I knew
stood for both Lord Alfred S. of Aspin Castle and his daughter
Angelica. Again, the letters are used for an unidentified man and
yet again for an unidentified woman. To add to the puzzle, I
found that by some obscure Gondalan convention father and
child did not always bear the same family name: a conversation
between a father and daughter, whom he addresses as Iernë, is
headed "I. M. to I. G." Confounding the confusion, Emily re-
duced groups and institutions, as well as personal names to in-
itials: "M. G. for the U. S." stands for "Mary Gleneden for the
Unique Society"; "The P. of I." for "The Palace of Instruction";
and "From a D—— W—— in the N. C." for "From a Dungeon
Wall in the North College."

The Angrian sequence had shown me how, as the plot grew,
situations altered and, particularly, how names changed with
marriage, territorial shifts, and acquisition of higher offices and
titles. In memory I counted no fewer than twenty familiar ap-
pellations for Angria's monarch, to say nothing of nicknames
and disguises, and a comparable number for his queen. I was
therefore less restrained by Emily's cryptic initials than I would
have been, lacking this analogy. I was conscious that every poem,
whether with or without identifying headings, must be tested by
consistency in plot, characterization, and emotional tone, as well
as by such internal evidence as personal names, place names, and
incident reference, before it could be accepted in pattern.

Narrative poems were helpful guideposts. "The Death of A.
G. A.," the most detailed in plot and dramatic in action of Emily's
poems, with its many retrospective passages and its tying to-
gether of plot threads in a climax of revenge, is in effect the key
to the theme and plot of the A. G. A.–Julius poems. Indeed, not
until this poem is reached in the reading does one become thor-
oughly aware of the compact unity of the group and feel intense
conviction of the Gondal world.

I spent uncounted hours in concentrated effort to think Emily's
thoughts and feel Emily's emotions after her. There were im-

passes of years' duration, such as I knew before I hit upon the connection between the three Geraldine poems ("Geraldine, the moon is shining"; "I knew not 'twas so dire a crime"; and " 'Twas night; her comrades gathered all") and A.G.A.'s poetic farewell to Lord Alfred ("Yes, holy be thy resting place").

As I worked I was more and more impressed with Emily's consistency in details, from the earliest of her poems (July 12, 1836) to the latest (May 13, 1848); from the introduction of her heroine as the child of Venus to her death as the victim of her star-mother's gifts; yet I found it well to keep in mind the seventeen years through which the epic grew, from 1831 to 1848, i.e., from Emily's fourteenth to thirtieth year. I knew from records of the Young Men's Play and from analogy to Angria, as well as from the birthday notes, that the plot was first played out orally with Anne, section by section and from day to day, then shaped into prose narratives, each girl writing independently of such incidents as she chose. But from Anne's poems it appears that the younger girls, unlike Charlotte and Branwell, used differing names for their common or parallel characters. The counterparts of Emily's A. G. A. and Julius, for instance, were presented by Anne under the more fanciful names Alexandria Zenobia and Alexander Hybernia. Composition dates indicate that Emily's poems, lagging months and in some cases years behind the plot development as set forth in the birthday notes, were by-products of her vanished prose.

I found, too, that allowance must be made for occasional lapses of Emily's memory in minor details, shifting of her poetic moods, and variations in her visions. Nor is Emily's poetic phraseology to be interpreted literally. In my early study I was tantalized, and no little puzzled, by the final stanza of "Lord of Elbë, on Elbë hill," which seemed to say that the lover in question, whom I knew to be dead, was gone on a long sea journey—

> But thou art now on a desolate sea
> Thinking of Gondal, and grieving for me;
> Longing to be in sweet Elbë again,
> Thinking and grieving and longing in vain.

—until I found a variant manuscript which reads,

> But thou are now on a desolate sea—
> Parted from Gondal and parted from me—
> All my repining is hopeless and vain,
> Death never yields back his victims again.

Again, in a poem headed "Rosina," Julius's grave is given as " 'mid northern mountains lone"; in "Cold in the earth, and the deep snow piled above thee," Rosina refers to it as "over the mountains on Angora's shore"; and the poem celebrating Rosina's coronation ("The organ swells, the trumpets sound") records that Julius "sleeps below," that is, in the "dark recesses" of the cathedral pavement.

The last major problem to be solved was the relation of Rosina and A. G. A., both queens of Gondal and dominant heroines of the epic. So alike they were in physical features and character that Miss Madeleine Hope Dodds, in her initial effort to work out the Gondal story, posited A. G. A. as the daughter of Rosina and Julius—but that was plainly impossible, as I proved to myself by working out the ages of the two at the time of Julius's assassination. With my first consecutive reading of all the then identified Gondal poems I began to suspect that Rosina and A. G. A. were one and the same. The two names gave me no pause, accustomed as I was to multiple names and titles for every character of the Young Men's Play and its Angrian expansion. If "two" queens did constitute one heroine, I reasoned, the connecting link was Julius, yet I found not a word associating him directly with A. G. A. His love life and political career seemed bound up wholly with Rosina of Alcona, as sweetheart, wife, and widow. My suspicion, or conviction, as it came to be, I found upon careful analysis, derived from Angelica's clear statement (in "The Death of A. G. A.") that her part in the assassination of Julius was motivated by revenge against A. G. A. At last the sought-for link flashed into mind—the three Julius-Geraldine poems, which at the same time gave me A. G. A.'s middle name, up to this point a mere initial. With these three women, Rosina, A. G. A. and Geraldine, reduced to one—Augusta Geraldine Almeda—the several groups of poems moved together in such a distinct and inevitable pattern, though broken by missing parts, that I could not doubt its correctness.

Others did doubt it, however, insisting that Rosina, A. G. A., and Geraldine were three distinct and separate persons. Then came the proof, clear and convincing as Euclid's first axiom. It came from an unexpected quarter—through a hitherto illegible manuscript belonging to the Fernando De Samara group, first deciphered by C. W. Hatfield, with Helen Brown and Joan Mott, and first printed in *Brontë Society Transactions*, 1938.

Fernando of Areon Hall, in Gaaldine, bade farewell to his sweetheart and foster sister in vows of eternal love. In Gondal he fell under the charms of A. G. A., and in complete infatuation for her cast away "virtue and faith and heaven." Tiring of his devotion, A. G. A. banished him to the "Gaaldine prison caves." In two poems headed "F. De Samara to A. G. A.," he curses her for her cruelty, at the same time confessing his hopeless, undying love for her. In a third poem he addresses himself to Alcona. Though this poem has no heading, the speaker identifies himself as Fernando by a reference to Areon Hall as his one-time home, and Alcona as A. G. A. by reiteration of his torturing, maddening love for her. It is plain, therefore, that A. G. A. is Alcona. But Rosina is Alcona. It follows then that A. G. A. and Rosina are one, unless, as Miss Dodds guessed, A. G. A. is the daughter of Rosina and Julius, inheriting her mother's territorial designation. A. G. A., however, cannot be Rosina's daughter, for the only daughter of whom we are told is born just before or just after Julius's assassination, whereas it is evident that A. G. A. is somewhat though not greatly older than her stepdaughter, Angelica, who in "The Death of A. G. A." identifies herself as one of the plotters of the assassination, making it clear that her motive was revenge against A. G. A. through Julius.

With proof that the two arch-heroines of Gondal are one, my conception of Emily Brontë's verse as an epic of Gondal narrowed to conviction that the great body of it was, more specifically, the life story of A. G. A., from dramatic birth, through tempestuous life, to tragic death.

Two prose bits casting light upon the relation of Emily's Gondal verse to her prose tend to confirm my conviction. On June 26,

1837, Emily, playing the Gondal game at Haworth with Anne, recorded that she was writing "Agustus [Augusta?] Almeda's life," and had about completed the first volume.[16] Unfortunately she does not say when she began the book, how long this volume was, or how many volumes were projected, but from her known speed of writing it is reasonable to suppose that this first volume had been in progress at least since July 12, 1836, the date when she set down on a single page of paper the four earliest of her extant poems: a girl child's birth stanza, the forecast of her life, and two incidents of her childhood. It would seem, then, that Emily's earliest poems were written concurrently with, or followed close upon, the opening chapters of Augustus Almeda's Life, and that they commemorate the birth and childhood of Gondal's heroine. By the date of this diary fragment (June 26, 1837), the number of poems had grown to thirteen. Eight years later, on July 31, 1845, Anne in her birthday note observes, "Emily is engaged in writing the Emperor Julius's life."[17] Dates of her last three distinctly Julius poems ("Cold in the earth, and the deep snow piled above thee," March 3, 1845; "Death, that struck when I was most confiding," April 10, 1845; and "Ah! why, because the dazzling sun," April 14, 1845) indicate that she had actually completed or was near completing the Life. When the diary fragment, the birthday note, and dates of earliest and latest poems are considered together, it is clear that the writing of the A. G. A.–Julius story in prose occupied, or spread itself over, nine years of Emily's life, i.e., from her eighteenth year to her twenty-seventh, a period coinciding with her A. G. A.–Julius verse.

Gaps in the story thread in Emily's poems and apparent detachment of some of the shorter pieces are explained by composition dates, which tell us that Emily was not in the verse itself creating a plot, or even following her prose consecutively, but merely highlighting such incidents and moods of the familiar Gondal world as stirred her imagination at the moment. The narrative of A. G. A.'s death (January, 1841–May, 1844), for instance, precedes a number of pivotal plot poems presenting the heroine in the freshness of youth and vigor of early maturity,

[16] See Appendix II. [17] See Appendix II.

such as the lament for Elbë ("O Day! He cannot die," December 2, 1844), written by A. G. A. in her early youth on prison walls of the Northern College, and her lament for Julius, spoken at the height of her power as reigning queen ("Cold in the earth, and the deep snow piled above thee," March 3, 1845). As will be seen in notes to the text, many sheets of Emily's manuscript verse carry several pieces each, bearing widely separated dates, which indicate again that Emily's poems were high points rising above the level of her continuous Gondal vision.

It is true that hardly half of Emily's 193 known poems and fragments are yet fitted accurately into the pattern, but there is nothing in those remaining outside to deny this thesis. The great majority of the indefinites are short vignettes of emotion—gladness, sorrow, remorse—probably connecting with the narrative poems we have or deriving from incidents of the Gondal Play recorded in her prose, but not repeated in verse. Many of them reflect A. G. A.'s personality—cast of mind, tone of voice, and turn of phrasing.

But A. G. A. and Julius, though a large part of the Gondal story, were not all of it. Emily and Anne's prose notes distinguish three periods of Gondal History: "The First Wars," from the founding of Gondal to the discovery and partitioning of Gaaldine among the princes of Gondal; the Julius-Rosina wars of aggression, from the marriage of Julius and Rosina to her death; and civil war between Republicans and Royalists. These periods correspond directly to Angrian history: wars with the Ashantees in conquest of the Glasstown country by the original Young Men; wars of conquest by which young Arthur Wellesley, Duke of Zamorna, expanded Glasstown into Angria with himself as emperor; and the Republican Revolution led by Alexander Percy. None of Emily's poems have been identified with the "First Wars," and but four with the Republican-Royalist conflict. Though the birthday notes of 1841 show that in the Gondal play itself clouds of civil war were even then lowering over the land, Emily's verse gives no hint of the situation until October 2, 1844, when a poem headed "D. G. C. to J. A." dramatized her earlier statement, "The Gondalians are at present in a threatening state, but there is no open rupture as yet." Nor did she return to the subject for almost a year, as she closed the A. G. A.-Julius period of Gondal's history in a burst of glorious poetry.

That the civil war theme had come to dominate the play long before it appears in the poems is revealed by both Emily and Anne on July 31, 1845: "The Royalists . . . are hard driven at present by the victorious Republicans," and "The Republicans are uppermost, but the Royalists are not quite overcome." Very soon, on an unspecified day in August following, Emily translated these conditions into the plaint of a young Royalist lying in "grave-like chill" "on the damp black flags of my dungeon-floor." Then, on October 9, 1845, she completed one of her best-known poems, headed "Julian M. and A. G. Rochelle" ("Silent is the House—all are laid asleep")—another prison picture, the victim a young girl.

How far Emily, uninterrupted, might have carried her verse chronicle of civil war in Gondal no one can say, but with this poem the spell was broken by Charlotte's discovery of her sister's notebook. "One day, in the autumn of 1845," Charlotte records, "I accidentally lighted on a MS. volume of verse in my sister Emily's handwriting. . . . I looked it over, and something more than surprise seized me,—a deep conviction that these were not common effusions, nor at all like the poetry women generally write. I thought them condensed and terse, vigorous and genuine. To my ear, they had also a peculiar music—wild, melancholy, and elevating. . . . It took hours to reconcile her to the discovery I had made, and days to persuade her that such poems merited publication."[18]

The outcome of Charlotte's discovery was an agreement among the three sisters to publish a joint volume of verse at their own expense, paying for it out of Aunt Elizabeth Branwell's legacy— twenty-one poems each, as the plan worked out. This decision made, Emily gave herself wholly to preparing her contributions. The work posed peculiar difficulties, for her best verse was marred for publication by strange names of persons and places, and her narratives were not of the familiar English world. With an effort at conformity hardly to be expected of her, she selected

[18] "Biographical Notice of Ellis and Acton Bell," *Wuthering Heights and Agnes Grey* (London, Smith, Elder and Company, 1850).

from the untitled notebook of 1844 fifteen poems having no be-
traying marks of their origin and from "Gondal Poems" six
pieces, bringing the latter into line by substituting general ti-
tles for identifying headings—"Edward" for "Elbë"; "Northern
shore" for "Angora's shore"; "Arden" for "Elnor"—and lifting
out of context stanzas from narrative poems. In all she altered,
shifted, or omitted ninety lines to change the nature and meaning
of these six poems.

Her part of the manuscript prepared, but before it went to
press, Emily, on January 2, 1846, set down as the last piece in her
untitled notebook, "No coward soul is mine." Though this poem,
probably her best-known, has been universally accepted as her
own sentiments, voiced in her own person, I am convinced that
it was spoken by a Gondalan facing a crisis incident to the civil
war.

Those who hold the traditional subjective interpretation of the
poems point to the fact that when Emily began transcribing her
verse in February, 1844, she set up two notebooks, designating
one as "Gondal Poems" and leaving the other without title, an
omission which, they believe, implies a deliberate distinction be-
tween Gondal poems and non-Gondal or subjective poems. Even
Mr. Hatfield, I think, was inclined to this opinion. The four cer-
tain Republican-Royalist poems were entered in "Gondal
Poems"; "No coward soul is mine" closes the untitled notebook.
To the minds of many this settles the question. But such reason-
ing ignores the fact that a fair proportion of poems in the untitled
volume are definitely of Gondal, though they have no identifying
headings and contain no personal or place names. "Death, that
struck when I was most confiding," for instance, is A. G. A.'s
anguished cry for Julius in the freshness of her grief, a brilliant
psychological companion piece to "Cold in the earth," her lament
for him after "fifteen wild Decembers" had dulled sharp pain to
continuous aching longing. Why Emily made the implied dis-
tinction, if it were a conscious distinction, can only be conjec-
tured. Remembering Charlotte's venture that a mind like her
sister's "could not be without some latent spark of honourable
ambition," I have guessed that Emily, knowing that her verse
was good but in its Gondal guise unintelligible to the public,

isolated those poems free of obvious Gondal limitation with fitness for publication in mind.

Charlotte in publishing "No coward soul is mine" in 1850 designated it as "the last lines my sister ever wrote." But Charlotte was mistaken. Nine months after writing it, and probably after she had finished *Wuthering Heights*, Emily returned to her epic, sketching in "Gondal Poems" a Republican-Royalist narrative of 263 lines, a poem of profound human insight and great dramatic power.

The publishing venture, a modest little volume designated simply as "*Poems* by Currer, Ellis, and Acton Bell," fell flat, and the girls drowned their disappointment in the novels they were writing, cast hopefully in English settings to find favor with a publisher.

Out of a second literary bid, based this time on their novels, came fame and financial independence for Charlotte, with *Jane Eyre*, and disappointment for Emily, when a shuddering public rejected *Wuthering Heights* as coarse and brutal. Again, on May 13, 1848, Emily turned to Gondal in revision of the unfinished civil war narrative of September 14, 1946, completing twenty-five lines which are actually, so far as the records go, her last written words.

In my conviction that all of Emily's verse, as we have it, falls within the Gondal context, I am not forgetting a small group of distinctly subjective pieces. These, more emphatically even than the narrative, reveal the dominating and directing influence of the Gondal creation in her life. They are eight in number.

The first, beginning "A little while, a little while" and carrying concrete images which stamp it as autobiographical, is a close parallel to Charlotte's occasional escapes from the grinding reality of Miss Wooler's school room to Angria. Davidson Cook on first seeing it in manuscript connected it with the Law Hill bondage days. With the choice before her of an hour's flight in spirit to Haworth Parsonage or Gondal—

> Shall I go there? or shall I seek
> Another clime, another sky,
> Where tongues familiar music speak
> In accent dear to memory?

—Emily chose Gondal's land of "bright, unclouded day," with "mountains circling every side," a "heaven" from which she could see "the wild moor-sheep feeding everywhere" and where she "marked out the tracks of wandering deer." This is indeed a subjective poem, but subjective in relation to Gondal.

Nature was Gondal's strongest rival for first place in Emily's heart. Three poems reflect the struggle: "In summer's mellow midnight" (September 11, 1840); "Shall Earth no more inspire thee" (May 16, 1841); and "Aye, there it is! It wakes to-night" (July 6, 1841). It is even more strongly emphasized in the poem "Often rebuked, yet always back returning," which Mr. Hatfield felt sure was written by Charlotte and included by her in the group of Emily's verse which she published in 1850, in an effort to interpret her sister to the public. Gondal won! And later poems testify how great was the victory. "My Comforter" ("Well hast thou spoken—and yet not taught," February 10, 1844) and "To Imagination" ("When weary with the long day's care," September 3, 1844) are poems of appreciation of Gondal as the medium of her burning genius, the only creative medium she yet knew. In glorious climax, on October 14 of the same year, she wrote in complete surrender her superb poem of adoration to Gondal as her "God of Visions" ("O thy bright eyes must answer now"):

> Thee, ever present, phantom thing—
> My slave, my comrade, and my King!

prophetically and tragically true, for when the public rejected *Wuthering Heights* she turned from Fame's altar-stone again to worship where "Faith cannot doubt nor Hope despair." Subjective? Yes, the very quintessence of Emily Brontë's genius, but a Gondal poem.

The scant outline we have of Emily's outward life abundantly reflects the controlling importance of Gondal to her health and happiness. When Charlotte and she, late in the summer of 1835, left Haworth Parsonage for Miss Wooler's school at Roe Head, Charlotte as teacher and Emily as pupil, both the Angrian and Gondalan games were at a crisis of excitement and suspense. The transfer from the exciting drama of their own familiar creations to the strange realities of school life was a severe shock to both sisters, comparable to the sundering of soul and body. Emily failed dismally to adjust herself. Her spirits drooped so low, that Charlotte, understanding, as no one else could, the cause of her sister's illness and fearing for her very life, "obtained her recall."

It was probably within the following half-year that Emily began "Augustus Almeda's Life." Her first poem, the A. G. A. birth-stanza, was written on or before July 12, 1836, about six months after her return. By the end of August, 1837, she had added to it twenty-six others of the now extant poems and fragments.

Her next venture from the parsonage was as teacher in Miss Patchett's school at Law Hill, under conditions which Charlotte characterized as "slavery": "My sister Emily is gone into a situation as teacher in a large school of near forty pupils, near Halifax. I have had one letter from her since her departure; it gives an appalling account of her duties—hard labor from six in the morning until near eleven at night, with only one half-hour of exercise between. This is slavery. I fear she will never stand it."[19] How long she remained in this post is variously estimated. If the poem "A little while, a little while" was written on the premises rather than in retrospect, she must have remained at Miss Patchett's at least up to the Christmas holidays of 1838. But this seems improbable, since about thirty per cent of her extant verse was composed between September 30, 1837, and December 18, 1838. Whatever the dates we accept for her departure and return, it is evident that she took Gondal to Law Hill with her, and from time to time found rest and refreshment in its familiar scenes.

It is evident, too, that Gondal went with her to Brussels, affording occasional escape from the strange busy alien life of Pensionnat Héger, for three poems, including "Written in Aspin Castle" ("How do I love on summer nights"), a pivotal Gondal narrative, bear dates between February and November, 1842, the period of her sojourn on the Continent. The year 1843, when she was alone in the parsonage with her father—Charlotte had returned to Brussels and Branwell and Anne were at Thorp Green—Emily

[19] Charlotte Brontë to Ellen Nussey, dated by Shorter, April 2, 1837, and by Symington, October 2, 1837.

produced fourteen poems, twelve of them accurately placed in the A. G. A. story. In the eighteen months between Charlotte's return from Brussels (January, 1844) and Branwell's dismissal from Thorp Green (July, 1845) there were thirteen, including "The Death of A. G. A.," a climactic narrative of 344 lines. In August following, amid the family distress of her brother's shameful return, she wrote a long Gondal poem headed "M. A. Written on the Dungeon Wall—N. C.," and on October 9, the Republican-Royalist narrative, "Julian M. and A. G. Rochelle." This date, October 9, 1845, I take as the day of Charlotte's discovery of Emily's manuscript notebook, for the poem is a long one, and it seems probable that Emily, interrupted in copying it, left the Gondal notebook out of place, where Charlotte found it. The untitled notebook shows no entry between June 2, 1845, and January 2, 1846.

After Charlotte's discovery, Emily added but two poems to the accumulation—the period from October, 1845, to January, 1848, belongs to her two literary excursions outside Gondal, *Poems* and *Wuthering Heights*. Cruel tragedies, both! These ordeals over, she turned again to Gondal with a final offering to her "God of Visions."

For all the world's adverse judgment of Emily's novel, Charlotte never wavered in conviction of her sister's genius, and, believing that the rejection of *Wuthering Heights* derived from devious dealings on the part of its publisher, Thomas Cautley Newby, she prepared, in 1850, a second edition to be brought out by her own publisher, Smith, Elder and Company. To it she joined eighteen of her Emily's poems not previously published, taking half the number from "Gondal Poems." Going considerably further than Emily herself had gone in adapting them to public taste, she not only made changes to disguise their origin, but ventured to "improve" whole lines and to add stanzas. C. W. Hatfield was convinced,[20] as mentioned earlier, that in her eagerness to interpret her sister to the world, she even included an entire poem of her own composition, the five stanzas beginning,

[20] Hatfield, *The Complete Poems of Emily Jane Brontë* (1941), pp. 5 and 254.

"Often rebuked, yet always back returning," expressing, he said, Charlotte's thoughts about her sister, but (in the first three verses) not what Emily would write about herself.

Whether Charlotte is to be praised for her good intentions or blamed for mistaken judgment, her efforts failed of their objective. Not even the combined popularity of Currer Bell and the prestige of Smith, Elder and Company could make Ellis Bell acceptable to her contemporaries. Emily's cousin, Eliza Jane Kingston, of Penzance, writing to her brother-in-law in America under date of March, 1860, probably reflected both the majority and minority opinion of *Wuthering Heights* in her remark, "I wish my cousin had never written 'Wuthering Heights,' although it is considered clever by some."

More than fifty years passed before Emily was again presented to the public in a volume of poems,[21] and then with an apologetic prefatory note, beginning with a quotation from Charlotte's introduction to the 1850 edition of *Wuthering Heights:*

"Usually it seems a sort of injustice to expose in print the crude thoughts of the unripe mind, the rude efforts of the unpracticed hand." . . . But since the manuscripts have been preserved, a few copies ought to be printed. Even such immature fragments, as most of these are, are of interest to the student and collector.

Other editions followed, three within twenty years, but it was not until 1941—nearly a century after Emily's death—that the public saw all her poems in one volume and as she wrote them, when C. W. Hatfield, working directly from her manuscripts, arranged the poems chronologically, restored their original headings, and made sure of every word of the text, starring nearly five hundred lines never before printed correctly. For fourteen poems,

---

[21] *Poems by Charlotte, Emily, and Anne Brontë Now for the First Time Printed* (New York, Dodd, Mead and Company, 1902). The edition was limited to 110 copies. To Emily fell the lion's share of space, with 67 poems against 10 by Charlotte and 12 by Anne.

The Prefatory Note in the University of Texas copy is signed by hand "L. S. L.," initials of Luther S. Livingston, at that time bibliographer for Dodd, Mead and Company. On the title page to Charlotte's poems is the manuscript note, "Transcribed from the original manuscripts by Mrs. Luther S. Livingston."

he was unable to find the author's manuscripts, and was forced to print from Shorter's transcripts.

It is to be regretted that Mr. Hatfield did not give his patient, meticulous interest to the Gondal story. With his broad knowledge and keen discernment he could, no doubt, have carried the reconstruction further than any other. That he did not is explained, I suspect, by his innate dislike of the unsure and unfinished. He was a perfectionist, and found no pleasure in reaching beyond his grasp—the immediately provable. He was also the personification of kindness and courtesy; it is probable that knowing my interest in the problem he generously restrained his own.

Happily for me, I am not a perfectionist. Though I knew that with the lost Gondal prose had gone the only possibility of a full understanding of Emily's genius, I have stubbornly followed the Gondal quest for a quarter of a century, lured on by distant landscapes, stirring events, mystical experiences, and the "wild, melancholy and elevating"music of Emily's verse. Stronger still has been the compulsion of sheer curiosity, which grows by each morsel of knowledge gained.

I have had disappointments, frustrations, and failures, but enough of success to repay my efforts, for I have penetrated further than I had reason to hope I might into the mysterious secret world created by Emily Brontë as an offering to her "God of Visions"; I have reconstructed in part two lost Emily Brontë novels; and I have glimpsed *Wuthering Heights* in the making. If another using the knowledge I have gathered and, I hope, correcting errors I may have made, can go beyond me and, perhaps, even fully map the still nebulous interior of the Gondal-Gaaldine world, I shall have no regrets that the privilege was not mine.

The plot-sequence of the poems and my own narrative prose links in the reconstruction here attempted are based on first-hand records, including all known literary remains of the four young Brontës. When inference or judgment must of necessity substitute for missing documents, I have checked it by every test that doubt and uncertainty can conjure up—derivation from or analogy to Glasstown and Angria, consistency with internal evidence, fitness in pattern, and Emily's known thoughts and habits.

The only questionable latitude I have allowed imagination is in the role assigned to Lord Eldred W.—his full name never appears—as astrologer and soothsayer. Even this assumption is justified by the scant evidence we have. In three of Emily's poems he appears by name, claiming lifelong devotion to A. G. A. and close identity with her shifting fortunes. In several he is recognized as the speaker or background figure, attending and guarding her, and it is not farfetched to identify him with the warning prophet in others. The world of the Young Men's Play was created and manipulated by magic. Its genii and other supernatural beings were modified in the Angrian stories to such Gothic realities as palace astrologers and statesmen gifted with "second sight." The role I have assigned Lord Eldred is in keeping with Gondal's descent from the Young Men's Play and its development as a parallel to Angria.

Gondal's Queen

A Novel in Verse by Emily Jane Brontë

The Argument

AUGUSTA GERALDINE ALMEDA or A. G. A., known also as Rosina, Princess of Alcona, a province in Gondal, was born under the predominating auspices of the planet Venus. From a "glorious child," loving and generous, courageous and truthful, a messenger of joy and gladness, she developed into a true daughter of her brilliant star, ardent in temperament, poetic in thought, fickle and changeable in love. Worshiped of all men who came under her charms, she brought tragedy to those upon whom her amorous light shone—death in battle to Lord Elbë; exile and death to Amedeus; exile and suicide to Lord Alfred; imprisonment, madness, and suicide to Fernando; assassination to Julius.

In Julius Brenzaida, Prince of Angora, A. G. A. found the one true and lasting passion of her life. Urged on by her ambition, and with her political and military help, he defeated his rivals, the princes of the House of Exina, treacherously making himself emperor of all Gondal and Gaaldine. At the height of his power he was assassinated by political and personal enemies led by Angelica, A. G. A.'s onetime stepdaughter, and by Angelica's foster brother, Amedeus, who together struck in revenge at A. G. A. through Julius.

With the overthrow of the Julian empire, A. G. A., or Rosina, became a fugitive with her child, whom she left to die in a mountain snowstorm. In time she rallied her forces and regained her throne, reigning brilliantly for fifteen years or longer, though grieving bitterly for Julius all the while.

One day her old enemy, Angelica, finding her upon the moors alone except for two unarmed attendants, lovers blindly absorbed in each other, incited Douglas, a fellow outlaw, to murder first the lovers and then the Queen herself. A. G. A.'s lifeless body was discovered by Lord Eldred, Captain of the Queen's Guard. Sending his men in pursuit of the assassin, he himself kept watch over the corpse, reviewing in thought the tempestuous career of this woman once "so adored, so deified," now lying "a wreck of desolate despair" in the moonlight before him.

Dramatis Personae

AUGUSTA GERALDINE ALMEDA
    variously designated as
    A. G. A.
    A. G. ALMEDA
    GERALDINE
    ROSINA
    ROSINA OF ALCONA
    ALCONA
Princess of Alcona, a province in Gondal, later Queen of Gondal, married successively Alexander, Lord of Elbë, Lord Alfred S. of Aspin Castle, and Julius Brenzaida.

JULIUS BRENZAIDA
    variously designated as
    ALMEDORE
    ANGORA
    J. A.
    J. B.
    KING JULIUS
    EMPEROR JULIUS
Prince of Angora, in Gondal, later King of Almedore, in Gaaldine, and Emperor of Gondal and Gaaldine.

ALEXANDRIA, infant daughter of A. G. A. and King Julius.

ALEXANDER, LORD OF ELBË
    variously designated as
    ALEXANDER
    ELBË
    A. E.
an early lover of A. G. A., killed in battle near Lake Elnor, in Gondal.

ALFRED S.
> also designated as
> LORD ALFRED
> A. S.

Lord of Aspin Castle, in Gondal, died an exile and suicide in England for love of A. G. A.

ANGELICA
> also designated as
> A. S. and perhaps as
> R. C.

daughter of Lord Alfred of Aspin Castle and the stepdaughter and enemy of A. G. A., helped plot the assassination of Julius, and instigated the murder of A. G. A.

AMEDEUS
> variously designated as
> A. A. A.
> H. A.
> A. E.

the "dark boy of sorrow" adopted by Angelica as her foster brother, became an outlaw and took part in the assassination of Julius, when he was himself killed.

FERNANDO DE SAMARA, one of the many victims of A. G. A.'s cruelty.

GLENEDEN, the ruling family of Exina, a province of Gondal:
> GERALD, the reigning prince, deposed and imprisoned by Julius Brenzaida; and

ARTHUR
E.
E. R. } relatives of Gerald.
MARY
R.

MARY R., sweetheart of E. Gleneden.

M. Douglas, lover of E. R. Gleneden.

DOUGLAS, Angelica's lover, an outlaw implicated in the assassination of Julius, and, at Angelica's persuasion, the murderer of A. G. A.

LORD ELDRED W., Captain of the Queen's Guard, her lifelong, faithful servant and the discoverer of her lifeless body.

Geographical Background

GONDAL, an island in the North Pacific, divided into four (or more) kingdoms:
    GONDAL
    ANGORA
    EXINA
    ALCONA
and having its federal capital at REGINA.

GAALDINE, an island in the South Pacific divided into kingdoms and provinces ruled by the royal families of Gondal:
    ALEXANDRIA
    ALMEDORE
    ELSERADEN
    ULA or ULAH, governed by four sovereigns
    ZELONA or ZALONA, with a city of the same name
    ZEDORA, a large province governed by a viceroy.

WERNA, a lake in Alcona, in Gondal.

ELNOR or ELMOR, a lake in Gondal, surrounded by Elmor (or Elnor) scars and moors.

ELDERNO, a lake in Gondal.

CHAPTER I

The Birth of a Princess

IN THE EARLY HOURS of a cold, clear winter morning a princess was born in the Royal Palace of Alcona, one of the four kingdoms which made up the rugged northern island of Gondal. There was no moon to light the landscape, but Venus, the brilliant morning star, looked down on her own image mirrored in the dark waters of nearby Lake Werna. Lord Eldred, the Palace astrologer and soothsayer, completing the child's horoscope, added on the same parchment her birth stanza, claiming her birthright as a daughter of Venus.

> Cold, clear, and blue, the morning heaven[1]
> Expands its arch on high;

[1] The manuscript of this vignette, without date of composition or identifying heading, is the first in order of four written on one side of a single small sheet, of which the second only bears a composition date, July 12, 1836, the earliest date found among Emily's poems. On the other side of the same sheet appear ten vignettes and fragments, the first of which is dated June, 1838. Because of these circumstances, Hatfield accepts "Cold, clear, and blue" as the earliest written of Emily's extant verse. Its place and function in the series does not become clear, however, until A. G. A.'s dominant place in the Gondal cycle has been established and the episodes of her strange career arranged in order; then it emerges in unmistakable clearness as the key to the heroine's complete character. This judgment is confirmed by the recent recovery of a journal fragment, dated July 26, 1837 (see Appendix II), which shows that the stanza was approximately coincident with the opening chapter of Emily's lost prose work, Augustus [Augusta?] Almeda's Life.

Cold, clear, and blue, Lake Werna's water
Reflects that winter's sky.
The moon has set, but Venus shines
A silent, silvery star.

On some significant summer day in the infant's life, perhaps
on her christening morn, the mother inquired of the soothsayer
the course of her child's life.

Will the day be bright or cloudy?[2]
Sweetly has its dawn begun;
But the heaven may shake with thunder
Ere the setting of the sun.

Lady, watch Apollo's journey:
Thus thy firstborn's course shall be—
If his beams through summer vapours
Warm the earth all placidly,
Her days shall pass like a pleasant dream in sweet tranquillity.

If it darken, if a shadow
Quench his rays and summon rain,
Flowers may open, buds may blossom:
Bud and flower alike are vain;
Her days shall pass like a mournful story in care and tears
and pain.

If the wind be fresh and free,
The wide skies clear and cloudless blue,
The woods and fields and golden flowers
Sparkling in sunshine and in dew,
Her days shall pass in Glory's light the world's drear desert
through.

Anxiously the royal mother watched the sky as early sunshine
gave way in midmorning to clouds, and clouds to gusty shower

[2] The manuscript of this poem, on the same page with "Cold, clear, and
blue," and following immediately after it, bears the date July 12, 1836,
the earliest found among Emily's poems. It has no identifying heading,
but its position and story content place it immediately after the birth
stanza, and the course of A. G. A.'s chequered career confirms the cor-
rectness of this arrangement.

dispersed in turn by dazzling sunshine, until afternoon showed, high up in the mountains, a gathering storm whose grimness was felt even within the curtained and carpeted bower. Then with determination that would not be denied the Queen ordered her ladies to fling wide the curtains from the windows, and she watched in tragic comprehension the majestic fury of the storm.

> High waving heather, 'neath stormy blasts bending,[3]
> Midnight and moonlight and bright shining stars;
> Darkness and glory rejoicingly blending,
> Earth rising to heaven and heaven descending,
> Man's spirit away from its drear dungeon sending,
> Bursting the fetters and breaking the bars.
>
> All down the mountain sides, wild forests lending
> One mighty voice to the life-giving wind;
> Rivers their banks in the jubilee rending,
> Fast through the valleys a reckless course wending,
> Wider and deeper their waters extending,
> Leaving a desolate desert behind.
>
> Shining and lowering and swelling and dying,
> Changing for ever from midnight to noon;
> Roaring like thunder, like soft music sighing,
> Shadows on shadows advancing and flying,
> Lightning-bright flashes the deep gloom defying,
> Coming as swiftly and fading as soon.

Fatalistically the mother accepted the omen,

> Woods, you need not frown on me;[4]
> Spectral trees, that so dolefully
> Shake your heads in the dreary sky,
> You need not mock so bitterly.

[3] This poem, dated December 13, 1836, has no identifying heading. In manuscript it shares a small sheet with three other pieces bearing one date, October, 1838. (See also, chap. II, note 5; chap. X, notes 7 and 11; chap. XI, note 2.) Its logical and dramatic connection with the preceding poems sets its place in the story.

[4] The manuscript of this vignette is on the same sheet with "High waving heather," immediately following it. Its place in the story is inferential.

CHAPTER II

Love Dawns

THE PRINCESS—Augusta Geraldine Almeda—grew and developed all too fast for those who hung on her every breath and would have prolonged the precious minutes of her childhood. Lord Eldred's heart swelled with pride and joy, as day by day realized the gracious promises of the stars at her birth.[1] Hers was a generous heart, courageous and truthful, "where love and gladness lay." Fresh and pure and free, she spread joy wherever she moved, even as she drew joy from all about her. "A glorious child" she was to him as he fondly read in her eyes "all virtues that ever honoured men."

It was his delight as Augusta's teacher to explore her young mind, joying in the originality of her fancies and the beauty of her speech. More often than she knew, her poetical figures put his mathematics and logic to rout, as on the day he attempted to introduce into her lesson a concept of time,

> Tell me, tell me, smiling child,[2]
> What the past is like to thee?
> "An Autumn evening soft and mild
> With a wind that sighs mournfully."

[1] See "E. W. to A. G. A." ("How few, of all the hearts that loved").

[2] This poem has no heading, but its position on the manuscript page, immediately following "Will the day be bright or cloudy?" which is dated July 12, 1836, together with its poetic figures—distinctly A. G. A.'s own, as they became abundantly familiar in succeeding poems—seems to place it with the early group pertaining to her childhood.

Tell me, what is the present hour?
"A green and flowery spray
    Where a young bird sits gathering its power
    To mount and fly away."

And what is the future, happy one?
"A sea beneath a cloudless sun;
    A mighty, glorious, dazzling sea
    Stretching into infinity."

In perfect health and joy she came to the age at which, by
Gondal custom and law, children of royal families were taken
under care of the state for instruction and training in govern-
ment.[3] Lord Eldred himself presented his pupil at the Southern
College or Palace of Instruction in Gaaldine, standing sponsor for
her past training and future advancement. Proudly he saw her
emerge from the initiation period as Rosina of Alcona, beloved
of her teachers and acknowledged leader among her fellow
students.[4] Only one in all the institution withheld homage—
Prince Julius of the House of Brenzaida, hitherto the favorite of
the college, its best student and most promising scholar. Ab-
sorbed in the pursuit of wisdom, he seemed hardly to see Rosina,
as he called her; certainly he did not see her with all his senses,
as others did.

To make him wholly conscious of her presence—her beauty,
her intelligence, her charm—became the object of her thoughts
and behavior. Absorbed in this determination, she neglected du-
ties. Knowledge lost its lure, and she gave herself to forbidden
pleasures, tempting Julius to join her.

O come with me, thus ran the song,[5]
The moon is bright in Autumn's sky,
And thou hast toiled and laboured long
With aching head and weary eye.

[3] Other Gondal poems and analogy to the Young Men's Play and the An-
grian stores. See Introduction, pp. 21, 22.

[4] Analogy to Charlotte's young Arthur Wellesley, Marquis of Douro.

[5] This poem is the last of three short fragments on one side of a single
manuscript sheet, the first of which, dated October, 1838, is headed "A. G.
A." This heading, joined to the content of the stanza, seems to indicate that
in it A. G. A. (Rosina) is addressing Julius.

For a time he resisted her allurements.

All day I've toiled, but not with pain,[6]
In learning's golden mine;
And now at eventide again
The moonbeams softly shine.

There is no snow upon the ground,
No frost on wind or wave;
The south wind blew with gentlest sound
And broke their icy grave.

'Tis sweet to wander here at night
To watch the winter die,
With heart as summer sunshine light
And warm as summer sky.

O may I never lose the peace
That lulls me gently now,
Though time should change my youthful face,
And years should shade my brow!

True to myself, and true to all,
May I be healthful still,
And turn away from passion's call,
And curb my own wild will.

In the end, however, Julius surrendered, subscribing to Ro-
sina's[7] nobly worded creed of pleasure and practicing it at the
expense of other obligations. Expostulations and rebukes failing
to bring him back to the path of duty, the elders of the college
meted out to him the severe penalty of solitary imprisonment in

[6] The manuscript of this poem has disappeared from sight. Hatfield
printed his text from Shorter's transcript—made prior to publication of
Complete Poems of Emily Brontë, 1910—which has neither date of com-
position nor identifying heading. Its content in connection with "Listen!
when your hair, like mine" suggests its place in the story, a suggestion
which is strengthened by Anne Brontë's companion poem ("The Student's
Serenade," February, 1844) signed "Alexander Hybernia." Alexander
Hybernia was Anne's Gondalan counterpart to Emily's Julius.

[7] For evidence that Rosina and A. G. A. are one, see Introduction, p. 26 f.
No certain explanation of the two names has been found; it may be that
Rosina was the name given her in the college initiation rites.

the College Dungeon. To pass the tedious hours, he wrote his story upon the damp, mouldy walls, bitterly questioning the sincerity and depth of Rosina's affection.

> "Listen! when your hair, like mine,[8]
>   Takes a tint of silver grey;
>   When your eyes, with dimmer shine,
>   Watch life's bubbles float away;
>
> "When you, young man, have borne like me,
>   The weary weight of sixty-three,
>   Then shall penance sore be paid
>   For these hours so wildly squandered;
>   And the words that now fall dead
> 10 On your ears, be deeply pondered;
>   Pondered and approved at last,
>   But their virtue will be past!
>
> "Glorious is the prize of Duty,
>   Though she be a serious power;
>   Treacherous all the lures of Beauty,
>   Thorny bud and poisonous flower!
>
> "Mirth is but a mad beguiling
>   Of the golden-gifted Time;
>   Love, a demon-meteor, wiling
> 20 Heedless feet to gulfs of crime.
>
> "Those who follow earthly pleasure,
>   Heavenly knowledge will not lead;
>   Wisdom hides from them her treasure,
>   Virtue bids them evil-speed!

[8] The manuscript of this poem, initialed "E. J. B." and dated November 11, 1844, has the identifying heading "From a Dungeon Wall in the Southern College. J. B. Sept., 1825." The internal date "Sept., 1825" is one of the four such dates found among Emily's poems. Apparently Southern College was in Gaaldine. Since Rosina and Julius were princes of both Gondal and Gaaldine, it was natural enough that they should attend the "Palace of Instruction" of Southern College and go home to Gondal for the long vacation. The familiar college dungeon of the Gondal poems was a relic from the Young Men's Play. See Introduction, pp. 12 ff., p. 21.

"Vainly may their hearts, repenting,
  Seek for aid in future years;
  Wisdom scorned knows no relenting;
  Virtue is not won by tears.

"Fain would we your steps reclaim,
30 Waken fear and holy shame.
  And to this end, our council well
  And kindly doomed you to a cell
  Whose darkness may, perchance, disclose
  A beacon-guide from sterner woes."

So spake my judge—then seized his lamp
And left me in the dungeon damp,
A vault-like place whose stagnant air
Suggests and nourishes despair!

Rosina, this had never been
40 Except for you, my despot queen!
  Except for you the billowy sea
  Would now be tossing under me,
  The wind's wild voice my bosom thrill
  And my glad heart bound wilder still,
  Flying before the rapid gale
  Those wondrous southern isles to hail
  Which wait for my companions free
  But thank your passion—not for me!

You know too well—and so do I—
50 Your haughty beauty's sovereignty;
  Yet have I read those falcon eyes—
  Have dived into their mysteries—
  Have studied long their glance and feel
  It is not love those eyes reveal.

They Flash, they burn with lightning shine,
But not with such fond fire as mine;
The tender star fades faint and wan
Before Ambition's scorching sun.
So deem I now—and Time will prove
60 If I have wronged Rosina's love.

CHAPTER III

Alexander, Lord of Elbë

JULIUS'S DOUBTS of Rosina's constancy were justified by her early elopement with Alexander, Lord Elbë, who deserted his young wife for her.[1] Through circumstances which do not appear, the forces of Elbë and Julius meet in battle near Lake Elnor, in Gondal. Elbë fell, mortally wounded, and was carried to a secluded spot at the edge of the lake to die.

> There swept adown that dreary glen[2]
> A wilder sound than mountain wind:
> The thrilling shouts of fighting men
> With something sadder far behind.

[1] This detail of the story is inferred from Anne Brontë's two-part poem "The Parting" ("The Chestnut stood by the gate"), signed "Alexandrina Zenobia, 1837," in which the Lord of Alzerno, bidding affectionate farewell to his young wife, Eliza, rides away never to return. Eliza's grief is accentuated by uncertainty of his fate. The narrator, Alexandrina Zenobia, talking with her three years after his departure, assures her that Alzerno is dead, for only death could keep him from her, confessing aside,

> But more than this I would not tell,
> Though all the while I knew so well
> The time and nature of his death;
> For when he drew his parting breath,
> His head was pillowed on my knee.

Since Alexandrina Zenobia is Anne's counterpart to Emily's A. G. A., or Rosina, one infers that Emily's vignette "None but one beheld him dying" is A. G. A.'s cryptic account of Elbë's death and, further, that A. G. A. eloped with Elbë as Alexandrina Zenobia eloped with Alzerno.

[2] The manuscript of this poem has neither date nor identifying heading,

The thrilling shouts they died away
Before the night came greyly down;
But closed not with the closing day
The choking sob, the tortured moan.

Down in a hollow sunk in shade
Where dark heath waved in secret gloom,
A weary bleeding form was laid
Waiting the death that was to come.

———

The battle had passed from the height,
And still did evening fall;
While heaven, with its hosts of night,
Gloriously canopied all.

The dead around were sleeping
On heath and granite grey;
And the dying their last watch were keeping
In the closing of the day.

———

How golden bright from earth and heaven
The summer day declines;
How gloriously o'er land and sea
The parting sunbeam shines.

There is a voice in the wind that waves
Those bright rejoicing trees.

———

Not a vapour had stained the breezeless blue,
Not a cloud had dimmed the sun
From the time of morning's earliest dew
Till the summer day was done;

And all as pure and all as bright
The beam of evening died;
And purer still its parting light
Shone in Lake Elnor's tide.

———

but it falls into place with convincing accuracy as the Elbë story unfolds
in successive poems. The five short poems and fragments that follow here
are among six on one side of a manuscript sheet dated August, 1837, and
almost certainly belong with it, as descriptive of the time, place, and at-
mosphere of Elbë's death.

Waveless and calm lies that silent deep
In its wilderness of moors;
Solemn and soft the moonbeams sleep
Upon its heathy shores.

The deer are gathered to their rest,
The wild sheep seek the fold.

Only some spires of bright green grass
Transparently in sunshine quivering.

The sun has set, and the long grass now
Waves drearily in the evening wind;
And the wild bird has flown from that old grey stone,
In some warm nook a couch to find.

In all the lonely landscape round
I see no sight and hear no sound,
Except the wind that far away
Comes sighing o'er the heathy sea.

There by Lake Elnor Augusta found him, and with his head in her lap, watched his life bleed itself away.

None but one beheld him dying,[3]
Parting with the parting day;
Winds of evening, sadly sighing,
Bore his soul from earth away.

Long afterward, Augusta, revisiting the scene, lived over in memory that terrible day.

There shines the moon, at noon of night[4]—
Vision of glory—Dream of light!

[3] This poem is eighth of the ten short vignettes on one manuscript sheet dated June, 1838. It has no identifying heading. (See chap. I, note 1.)

[4] The manuscript of this poem, dated March 6, 1837, has the identifying heading "A. G. A.," which is the earliest heading found among Emily's poems. It is also the first occurrence of the heroine's name or initials in any form. The text reveals that the first letter stands for Augusta; later poems complete the name as Augusta Geraldine Almeda.

Holy as heaven—undimmed and pure,
Looking down on the lonely moor—
And lonelier still beneath her ray
That drear moor stretches far away
Till it seems strange that aught can lie
Beyond its zone of silver sky.

Bright moon—dear moon! when years have past
10 My weary feet return at last—
And still upon Lake Elnor's[5] breast
Thy solemn rays serenely rest
And still the fern-leaves sighing wave
Like mourners over Elbë's grave
And Earth's the same but oh to see
How wildly Time has altered me!
Am I the being who long ago
Sat watching by that water side,
The light of life expiring slow
20 From his fair cheek and brow of pride?
Not oft these mountains feel the shine
Of such a day—as, fading then,
Cast from its fount of gold divine
A last smile on the heathery plain,
And kissed the far-off peaks of snow
That gleaming on the horizon shone
As if in summer's warmest glow
Stern winter claimed a loftier throne—
And there he lay among the bloom
30 His red blood dyed a deeper hue,
Shuddering to feel the ghostly gloom
That coming Death around him threw—
Sickening to think one hour would sever
The sweet, sweet world and him for ever,
To think that twilight gathering dim
Would never pass away to him—
No—never more! That awful thought
A thousand dreary feelings brought,
And memory all her powers combined
40 And rushed upon his fainting mind.

[5] Also written Elmor.

Wide, swelling woodlands seemed to rise
Beneath soft, sunny southern skies—
Old Elbë Hall, his noble home,
Towered 'mid its trees, whose foliage green
Rustled with the kind airs that come
From summer heavens when most serene,
And bursting through the leafy shade
A gush of golden sunshine played,
Bathing the walls in amber light
50 And sparkling in the water clear
That stretched below—reflected bright
The whole wide world of cloudless air—
And still before his spirit's eye
Such well-known scenes would rise and fly
Till, maddening with despair and pain
He turned his dying face to me
And wildly cried, "Oh, once again
Might I my native country see!
But once again—one single day!—
60 And must it—can it *never* be?
To die—and die so far away
When life has hardly smiled for me.
Augusta[6]—you will soon return
Back to that land in health and bloom
And then the heath alone will mourn
Above my unremembered tomb,
For you'll forget the lonely grave
And mouldering corpse by Elnor's wave."

Julius, finding Rosina alone with her dead lover, gave her
sorely needed assistance, but when she would have presumed on
his former devotion, he repelled her in cold and scornful pride.

Why do I hate that lone green dell?[7]
Buried in moors and mountains wild,
That is a spot I had loved too well
Had I but seen it when a child.

[6] The name Augusta occurs but once again in the Gondal poems, in "The
Death of A. G. A." ("Were they shepherds, who sat all day").
[7] The manuscript of this poem, dated May 9, 1838, bears the identifying
heading "A. G. A."

[59

There are bones whitening there in the summer's
　　heat,
But it is not for that, and none can tell;
None but one can the secret repeat
Why I hate that lone green dell.

Noble foe, I pardon thee
All thy cold and scornful pride,
For thou wast a priceless friend to me
When my sad heart had none beside.

And, leaning on thy generous arm,
A breath of old times over me came;
The earth shone round with a long-lost charm;
Alas, I forgot I was not the same.

Before a day—an hour—passed by,
My spirit knew itself once more;
I saw the gilded vapours fly
And leave me as I was before.

Exactly one year from the time Julius wrote his accusation of
Rosina on the prison wall of the Southern College, Rosina—or
Augusta—herself was inscribing on a dungeon wall of the North-
ern College a heartbreaking dirge for Elbë.

"O Day! He cannot die[8]
When thou so fair art shining;
O Sun! in such a glorious sky
So tranquilly declining,

[8] The manuscript of this poem is dated December 2, 1844, seven months
after "The Death of A. G. A." was completed. It bears the identifying
heading "A. G. A. Sept., 1826 From a D——W——in the N. C." [From a
Dungeon Wall in the Northern College]. "Sept., 1826," is one of the four
dates denoting internal Gondalan chronology found in Emily's poems. Ap-
parently it was inserted to emphasize the connection of this poem with
Julius's plaint written on the Dungeon Wall of the Southern College
"Sept., 1825," and the swift retribution visited on A. G. A. as the cause of
his imprisonment.
　　A. G. A. does not specify the imprisoning authority. Presumably it was
the same (or a similar college council) as that quoted by Julius, and the
punishment was meted out for an offense similar to his and in the same
hope—reclamation from a self-willed and pleasure-loving life.

"He cannot leave thee now
　While fresh west-winds are blowing,
　And all around his youthful brow
　Thy cheerful light is glowing!

"Elbë, awake, awake!
10　The golden evening gleams
　Warm and bright on Elnor's lake,
　Arouse thee from thy dreams!

"Beside thee, on my knee,
　My dearest friend, I pray
　That thou, to cross the eternal sea
　Wouldst yet *one* hour delay!

"I hear its billows roar,
　I see them foaming high,
　But no glimpse of a further shore
20　Has blessed my straining eye.

"Believe not what they urge
　Of Eden isles beyond;
　Turn back, from that tempestuous surge,
　To thy own native land!

"It is not Death, but pain
　That struggles in thy breast;
　Nay, rally, Elbë, rouse again,
　I cannot let thee rest!"

One long look, that sore reproved me
30　For the woe I could not bear—
　One mute look of suffering moved me
　To repent my useless prayer;

And with sudden check, the heaving
　Of distraction passed away;
　Not a sign of further grieving
　Stirred my soul that awful day.

Paled at last, that sweet sun setting;
　Sank to peace the gentle breeze;
　Summer dews fell softly, wetting
40　Glen and glade, and silent trees.

Then his eyes began to weary,
Weighed beneath a mortal sleep;
And their light grew strangely dreary,
Clouded, even as they would weep;

But they wept not, but they changed not,
Never moved and never closed;
Troubled still, and still they ranged not,
Wandered not, nor yet reposed!

So I knew that he was dying—
50 Stooped and raised his languid head—
Felt no breath and heard no sighing,
So, I knew that he was dead.

Through the terrible days, weeks, and months that followed,
Augusta forgot her grief for Elbë in her own misery, as the horrors of prison drove her to the verge of madness.

O transient voyager of heaven![9]
O silent sign of winter skies!
What adverse wind thy sail has driven
To dungeons where a prisoner lies?

Methinks the hands that shut the sun
So sternly from this mourning brow
Might still their rebel task have done
And checked a thing so frail as thou.

They would have done it had they known
The talisman that dwelt in thee,
For all the suns that ever shone
Have never been so kind to me.

For many a week, and many a day,
My heart was weighed with sinking gloom,
When morning rose in mourning grey
And faintly lit my prison room;

[9] The manuscript of this poem, signed "Emily Jane Brontë, December
——, 1837," has the identifying heading "To a Wreath of Snow By A. G.
Almeda." This is the first and only occurrence of the heroine's surname in
the series. It is in two poems dated almost a year later, October 17, 1838,
that her middle name, Geraldine, appears.

But, angel like, when I awoke,
Thy silvery form so soft and fair,
Shining through darkness, sweetly spoke
Of cloudy skies and mountains bare—

The dearest to a mountaineer,
Who, all life long has loved the snow
That crowned her[10] native summits drear
Better than greenest plains below.

And, voiceless, soulless messenger,
Thy presence waked a thrilling tone
That comforts me while thou art here
And will sustain when thou art gone.

Free at last, A. G. A. sailed for Gaaldine, joying in freedom as
only one of her nature could joy after prison torture.

O God of heaven! the dream of horror,[11]
The frightful dream is over now;
The sickened heart, the blasting sorrow,
The ghastly night, the ghastlier morrow,
The aching sense of utter woe;

The burning tears that would keep welling,
The groans that mocked at every tear
That burst from out their dreary dwelling
As if each gasp were life expelling,
10 But life was nourished by despair;

The tossing and the anguished pining;
The grinding teeth and staring eye;
The agony of still repining,

[10] In all printings of this poem before Hatfield's edition, *her* was printed
as *his*, though the word is clear enough in the manuscript.
[11] The manuscript of this poem, dated August 7, 1837 and initialed
"E. J. B." (twelve days after Emily's journal fragment stating that she was
about to complete the first volume of Augustus Almeda's Life), has no
identifying heading, but text and tone place it accurately in the A. G. A.
story. It is interesting to compare A. G. A.'s reaction to imprisonment with
that of two other young women of Emily's poems: "Iernë's eyes were
glazed and dim," no date or identifying heading (see Appendix I, note 4);
and "Julian M. and A. G. Rochelle" ("Silent is the house"), October 9,
1845 (see Appendix I).

When not a spark of hope was shining
From gloomy fate's relentless sky;

The impatient rage, the useless shrinking
From thoughts that yet could not be borne;
The soul that was for ever thinking,
Till nature, maddened, tortured, sinking,
20 At last refused to mourn—

It's over now—and I am free,
And the ocean wind is caressing me,
The wild wind from that wavy main
I never thought to see again.

Bless thee, Bright Sea—and glorious dome,
And my own world, my spirit's home;
Bless thee, Bless all—I can not speak:
My voice is choked, but not with grief;
And salt drops from my haggard cheek
30 Descend, like rain upon the heath.

How long they've wet a dongeon floor,
Falling on flag-stones damp and grey!
I used to weep even in my sleep;
The night was dreadful, like the day.

I used to weep when winter's snow
Whirled through the grating stormily,
But then it was a calmer woe
For everything was drear as me.

The bitterest time, the worst of all,
40 Was that in which the summer sheen
Cast a green luster on the wall
That told of fields of lovelier green.

Often I've sat down on the ground,
Gazing up to that flush scarce seen,
Till, heedless of the darkness round,
My soul has sought a land serene.

It sought the arch of heaven divine,
The pure blue heaven with clouds of gold;
It sought thy father's home and mine
50 As I remembered it of old.

O even now too horribly
Come back the feelings that would swell,
When with my face hid on my knee
I strove the bursting groans to quell.

I flung myself upon the stone,
I howled and tore my tangled hair,
And then, when the first gush had flown,
Lay in unspeakable despair.

Sometimes a curse, sometimes a prayer
60 Would quiver on my parchèd tongue;
But both without a murmur there
Died in the breast from whence they sprung.

And so the day would fade on high,
And darkness quench that lonely beam,
And slumber mould my misery
Into some strange and spectral dream
Whose phantom horrors made me know
The worst extent of human woe—

But this is past, and why return
70 O'er such a past to brood and mourn?
Shake off the fetters, break the chain,
And live and love and smile again.

The waste of youth, the waste of years,
Departed in that dongeon's thrall;
The gnawing grief, the hopeless tears,
Forget them—O forget them all.

At one of her family homes, apparently in Gaaldine, while her strong young body and mind recuperated from her harrowing experiences, Augusta faced the realization that Elbë had passed out of her life.

Lord of Elbë, on Elbë hill[12]
The mist is thick and the wind is chill
And the heart of thy Friend from the dawn of day
Has sighed for sorrow that thou went away.

[12] There are two manuscripts of this entire poem, both dated August 19, 1837, showing interesting variation in single lines. The first, initialed

Lord of Elbë, how pleasant to me
The sound of thy blithesome step would be
Rustling the heath that, only now
Waves as the night-gusts over it blow.

Bright are the fires in thy lonely home
I see them far off, and as deepens the gloom
Gleaming like stars through the high forest-boughs
Gladder they glow in the park's repose.

O Alexander![13] when I return,
Warm as those hearths my heart would burn,
Light as thine own, my foot would fall
If I might hear thy voice in the hall.

But thou art now on a desolate sea—[14]
Parted from Gondal and parted from me—
All my repining is hopeless and vain,
Death never yields back his victims again.

O come again; what chains withhold[15]
The steps that used so fleet to be?
Come, leave thy dwelling dank and cold
Once more to visit me.

Was it with the fields of green,
Blowing flower and budding tree,
With the summer heaven serene,
That thou didst visit me?

"E.," has the identifying heading "A. G. A. to A. E."; the second is headed "Song   A. G. A." There is also a third manuscript of the last five lines, signed and dated at the end, "E. J. Bronte"—August 19, 1837."

[13] Alexander Elbë.

[14] Variant stanza.

> But thou art now on the desolate sea
> Thinking of Gondal, and grieving for me;
> Longing to be in sweet Elbë again,
> Thinking and grieving and longing in vain.

[15] This and the following piece are among seven undated short poems without headings written on one side of a single sheet of paper; the reverse side carrying three poems is dated March, 1838.

> No; 'twas not the flowery plain;
> No; 'twas not the fragrant air:
> Summer skies will come again,
> But *thou* wilt not be there.

The sharpness of early grief gave way in time to romantic memories.

> Coldly, bleakly, drearily,[16]
> Evening died on Elbë's shore;
> Winds were in the cloudy sky,
> Sighing, mourning evermore.

> Old Hall of Elbë, ruined, lonely now;
> House to which the voice of life shall never more return;
> Chambers roofless, desolate, where weeds and ivy grow;
> Windows through whose broken arches the night-winds
>   sadly mourn;
> Home of the departed, the long-departed dead.

Along with physical health returned A. G. A.'s characteristic optimism and will to happiness.

> What use is it to slumber here,[17]
> Though the heart be sad and weary?
> What use is it to slumber here,
> Though the day rise dark and dreary?

> For that mist may break when the sun is high,
> And this soul forget its sorrow;
> And the rosy ray of the closing day
> May promise a brighter morrow.

------

[16] This poem and the following vignette have no identifying headings. They are the last two of the ten short poems and fragments on one manuscript sheet dated at the top of recto, June, 1838.

[17] This poem and the following one are among the seven short pieces referred to in note 15, above. Their only identification is fitness in the story pattern.

Here, with my knee upon thy stone,[18]
I bid adieu to feelings gone;
I leave with thee my tears and pain,
And rush into the world again.

[18] The occasion of this stanza may be Augusta's visit to the scene of Elbë's death, as related in "There shines the moon, at noon of night."

CHAPTER IV

The Lady of Aspin Castle

IN TIME A. G. A. was deep in another love adventure. Even
more ardently than to Alexander, Lord of Elbë, she now gave
her love to Lord Alfred S. of Aspin Castle, with protestations of
eternal faithfulness.

> At such a time, in such a spot,[1]
> The world seems made of light;
> Our blissful hearts remember not
> How surely follows night.

> I cannot, Alfred, dream of aught
> That casts a shade of woe;
> That heaven is reigning in my thought,
> Which wood and wave and earth have caught
> From skies that overflow.

[1] The manuscript of this poem is signed "E." and bears dates of begin-
ning and completion, May 6, 1840—July 28, 1843, showing that it was
more than three years in writing, a period which included Emily's sojourn
in Brussels. It is headed "A. G. A. to A. S." The text supplies the given name
Alfred. It has been suggested that Lord Alfred's family name was Sidonia,
from the line "There stands Sidonia's deity," in "Written in Aspin Castle"
("How do I love on summer nights"). It seems more likely, however, that
"Sidonia" is used as a figure of speech to suggest Augusta's beauty and
cruelty, i.e., she was as beautiful and heartless as the Sidonian deity,
Astarte, or Ashtaroth. Charlotte's poem "Gods of the old mythology" re-
veals that the parsonage girls were familiar with the names and character-
istics of heathen gods, including Ashtaroth by name.

The story of A. G. A. and Lord Alfred is continued in "Written in Aspin
Castle" and "The Death of A. G. A." ("Were they shepherds").

10 That heaven which my sweet lover's brow
   Has won me to adore,
   Which from his blue eyes beaming now
   Reflects a still intenser glow
   Than nature's heaven can pour.

   I know our souls are all divine;
   I know that when we die,
   What seems the vilest, even like thine
   A part of God himself shall shine
   In perfect purity.

20 But coldly breaks November's day;
   Its changes, charmless all;
   Unmarked, unloved, they pass away;
   We do not wish one hour to stay,
   Nor sigh at evening's fall.

   And glorious is the gladsome rise
   Of June's rejoicing morn;
   And who with unregretful eyes
   Can watch the lustre leave its skies
   To twilight's shade forlorn?

30 Then art thou not my golden June
   All mist and tempest free?
   As shines earth's sun in summer noon
   So heaven's sun shines in thee.

   Let others seek its beams divine
   In cell and cloister drear;
   But I have found a fairer shrine
   And happier worship here.

   By dismal rites they win their bliss—
   By penance, fasts, and fears;
40 I have one rite: a gentle kiss;
   One penance: tender tears.

   O could it thus forever be
   That I might so adore;
   I'd ask for all eternity
   To make a paradise for me,
   My love—and nothing more!

Lord Alfred had a daughter of almost divine beauty, the child of an earlier marriage,[2] fittingly called Angelica from her golden hair and blue eyes, just like her father's own.[3] Once the idol of his heart, Angelica found herself all but forgotten in his devotion to Augusta, but little she cared, for she, too, gave her heart's worship at the same shrine.[4]

Among the young people of Angelica's circle was a boy of dark and tragic aspect, doomed to sorrow from his birth.[5]

> I saw thee, child, one summer's day[6]
> Suddenly leave thy cheerful play,
> And in the green grass, lowly lying,
> I listened to thy mournful sighing.
>
> I knew the wish that waked that wail;
> I knew the source whence sprung those tears;
> You longed for fate to raise the veil
> That darkened over coming years.
>
> The anxious prayer was heard, and power
> 10 Was given me, in that silent hour,
> To open to an infant's eye
> The portals of futurity.
>
> But, child of dust, the fragrant flowers,
> The bright blue sky and velvet sod
> Were strange conductors to the bowers
> Thy daring footsteps must have trod.

[2] Recorded, possibly, in the poem, "Where beams the sun the brightest," headed in manuscript, "To A. S., 1830" (see Hatfield, *The Complete Poems* [1941], p. 186). Here again the date refers to internal Gondal chronology.

[3] "Written in Aspin Castle" ("How do I love on summer nights"), lines 61–74.

[4] "The Death of A. G. A." ("Were they shepherds"), lines 63–80.

[5] The prototype of Heathcliff in *Wuthering Heights*, just as Angelica in her happy childhood is the prototype of Cathy.

[6] The manuscript of this poem, dated July, 1837, has no identifying heading, but its fated child is unmistakable. The identity of the spirit-narrator is made the more puzzling by the fact that the recto of the same sheet carries another poem, "The night of storms has passed," (June 10, 1837), in which appears the same or another specter to warn the speaker, who seems to be Lord Eldred, of the coming assassination of Emperor Julius.

I watched my time, and summer passed,
And Autumn waning fleeted by,
And doleful winter nights at last
20 In cloudy mourning clothed the sky.

And now I'm come: this evening fell
Not stormily, but stilly drear;
A sound sweeps o'er thee like a knell
To banish joy and welcome care;

A fluttering blast that shakes the leaves,
And whistles round the gloomy wall,
And lingering long lamenting grieves,
For 'tis the spectre's call.

He hears me: what a sudden start
30 Sent the blood icy to that heart;
He wakens, and how ghastly white
That face looks in the dim lamplight.

Those tiny hands in vain essay
To thrust the shadowy fiend away;
There is a horror on his brow,
An anguish in his bosom now;

A fearful anguish in his eyes
Fixed strainedly on the vacant air;
Heavily bursts in long-drawn sighs
40 His panting breath, enchained by fear.

Poor child, if spirits such as I
Could weep o'er human misery,
A tear might flow, aye, many a tear,
To see the road that lies before,
To see the sunshine disappear,
And hear the stormy waters roar,
Breaking upon a desolate shore,
Cut off from hope in early day,
From power and glory cut away.

50 But it is doomed, and morning's light
Must image forth the scowl of night,
And childhood's flower must waste its bloom
Beneath the shadow of the tomb.

Shadows closed around this unhappy boy until, at eighteen years of age, he felt himself without a friend in the world.

I am the only being whose doom[7]
No tongue would ask, no eye would mourn;
I never caused a thought of gloom,
A smile of joy, since I was born.

In secret pleasure, secret tears,
This changeful life has slipped away,
As friendless after eighteen years,
As lone as on my natal day.[8]

There have been times I cannot hide,
There have been times when this was drear,
When my sad soul forgot its pride
And longed for one to love me here.

But those were in the early glow
Of feelings since subdued by care;
And they have died so long ago,
I hardly now believe they were.

First melted off the hope of youth,
Then fancy's rainbow fast withdrew;
And then experience told me truth
In mortal bosoms never grew.

'Twas grief enough to think mankind
All hollow, servile, insincere;
But worse to trust to my own mind
And find the same corruption there.

[7] The manuscript of this poem has disappeared from sight. The text and date (May 17, 1837) are taken from Shorter's transcript as published in 1910. The speaker is recognized, however, as the ill-fated child of the preceding poem, now approaching manhood.

[8] Compare Nelly Dean's statement about Catherine Linton's newborn child, Cathy II: "An unwelcomed infant it was, poor thing! . . . its beginning was as friendless as its end is likely to be."

Angelica's warm, tender young heart, pitying this lonely and wretched boy, reached out and drew him into her loving care.

Heavy hangs the raindrop[9]
From the burdened spray;
Heavy broods the damp mist
On uplands far away;

Heavy looms the dull sky,
Heavy rolls the sea—
And heavy beats the young heart
Beneath that lonely tree.

Never has a blue streak
10 Cleft the clouds since morn—
Never has his grim Fate
Smiled since he was born.

Frowning on the infant,
Shadowing childhood's joy,
Guardian angel knows not
That melancholy boy.

Day is passing swiftly
Its sad and sombre prime;
Youth is fast invading
20 Sterner manhood's time.

All the flowers are praying
For sun before they close,

[9] The manuscript of this poem and its companion, following, is dated May 28, 1845, and carries the identifying heading "A. E. and R. C." A. E. is clearly the dark boy of sorrow again, at the same age as in the preceding poem. The name for which A. E. stands never comes clear. In "The Death of A. G. A." Angelica calls this dark boy "my Amedeus," but there is no indication whether Amedeus is his actual name or Angelica's endearing name for him. The girl's initials, R. C., offer even greater problems. From "The Death of A. G. A." it seems clear that this "child of delight" is Angelica, daughter of Lord Alfred S., but on what basis she would be designated as R. C. does not appear. Possibly Angelica was her pet name, while R. C. was her real name. As mentioned in the Introduction, multiple designations for the same person are frequent, a custom beginning with the Young Men's Play.

The suggestion of Heathcliff and Cathy of *Wuthering Heights* in these two poems is obvious.

And he prays too, unknowing,
That sunless human rose!

Blossoms, that the west wind
Has never wooed to blow,
Scentless are your petals,
Your dew as cold as snow.

Soul, where kindred kindness
30 No early promise woke,
Barren is your beauty
As weed upon the rock.

Wither, Brothers, wither,
You were vainly given—
Earth reserves no blessing
For the unblessed of Heaven!

Child of Delight! with sunbright hair,
And seablue, seadeep eyes;
Spirit of Bliss, what brings thee here,
Beneath these sullen skies?

Thou shouldest live in eternal spring,
Where endless day is never dim;
Why, seraph, has thy erring wing
Borne thee down to weep with him?

"Ah, not from heaven am I descended,
And I do not come to mingle tears;
But sweet is day, though with shadows blended;
And, though clouded, sweet are youthful years.

"I, the image of light and gladness,
Saw and pitied that mournful boy,
And I swore to take his gloomy sadness,
And give to him my beamy joy.

"Heavy and dark the night is closing;
Heavy and dark may its biding be:
Better for all from grief reposing,
And better for all who watch like me.

"Guardian angel, he lacks no longer;
Evil fortune he need not fear:
Fate is strong, but Love is stronger;
And more unsleeping than angel's care."

Youthful affection between Amedeus and Angelica ripened into romantic love. Lord Eldred, seeing them in a love embrace, was reminded of a similar scene from years gone by, and with a seer's vision forecast the tragedy awaiting them.

In the same place, when Nature wore[10]
The same celestial glow,
I'm sure I've seen those forms before
But many springs ago;

And only *he* had locks of light,
And *she* had raven hair;
While now, his curls are dark as night,
And hers as morning fair.

Besides, I've dreamt of tears whose traces
10 Will never more depart,
Of agony that fast effaces
The verdure of the heart.

I dreamt one sunny day like this,
In this peerless month of May,
I saw her give the unanswered kiss
As his spirit passed away:

Those young eyes that so sweetly shine
Then looked their last adieu,
And pale Death changed that cheek divine
20 To his unchanging hue;

And earth was cast above the breast
That beats so warm and free

[10] The manuscript of this poem, dated May 17, 1842, when Emily was studying in Brussels, has the identifying heading "H. A. and A. S." Obviously, both by recognition and from the later story pattern, the embracing dark-haired boy and golden-haired girl are Amedeus and Angelica, though information interpreting the initials H. A. is lacking.

Where her soft ringlets lightly rest
And move responsively.

Then she, upon the covered grave—
The grass grown grave, did lie:
A tomb not girt by Gondal's wave
Nor arched by Gondal's sky.

The sod was sparkling bright with dew,
30 But brighter still with tears,
That welled from mortal grief, I knew,
Which never heals with years.

And if he came not for her woe,
He would not now return;
He would not leave his sleep below
When she had ceased to mourn.

O Innocence, that cannot live
With heart-wrung anguish long—
Dear childhood's Innocence, forgive,
40 For I have done thee wrong!

The bright rose-buds, those hawthorns shroud
Within their perfumed bower,
Have never closed beneath a cloud,
Nor bent before a shower—

Had darkness once obscured their sun
Or kind dew turned to rain,
No storm-cleared sky that ever shone
Could win such bliss again.

The earlier lovers whom Lord Eldred sees in memory may
have been Lord Alfred and A. G. A.—"*he* had locks of light, *she*
had raven hair," but the emphasis on the season, May, possibly
refers to an unidentified guilty love affair of which A. G. A.
herself tells.

O wander not so far away![11]
O love, forgive this selfish tear—
It may be sad for thee to stay,
But how can I live lonely here?

[11] The manuscript of this poem, initialed "E." and dated May 20, 1838,
is headed "A. G. A. to A. S."

The still May morn is warm and bright,
Young flowers look fresh and grass is green;
And in the haze of glorious light
Our long, low hills are scarcely seen.

The woods—even now their small leaves hide
The blackbird and the stockdove well;
And high in heaven, so blue and wide,
A thousand strains of music swell.

He looks on all with eyes that speak
So deep, so drear a woe to me!
There is a faint red on his cheek
Not like the bloom I used to see.

Call Death—yes, Death, he is thine own!
The grave must close those limbs around,
And hush, for ever hush the tone
I loved above all earthly sound.

Well, pass away with the other flowers:
Too dark for them, too dark for thee
Are the hours to come, the joyless hours,
That Time is treasuring up for me.

If thou hast sinned in this world of care,
'Twas but the dust of thy drear abode—
Thy soul was pure when it entered here,
And pure it will go again to God.

Amedeus, like Angelica, gave Augusta, "Lord Alfred's idol
queen," eager affection. She, on her part, following the impulse
of her nature, led him on into passionate love, until, having
broken his honor and finding his attention boresome, she sent
him into exile, excusing herself in noble poetic words.[12]

Sleep not, dream not; this bright day[13]
Will not, cannot last for aye;
Bliss like thine is bought by years
Dark with torment and with tears.

[12] See also "The Death of A. G. A.," lines 81–99.
[13] This manuscript, undated, is headed, "A. A. A.," initials which seem to
stand for a form of Amedeus's name. The speaker is recognized as A. G. A.
by the poetic language of her self-excuse.

Sweeter far than placid pleasure,
Purer, higher, beyond measure,
Yet alas the sooner turning
Into hopeless, endless mourning.

I love thee, boy; for all divine,
All full of God thy features shine.
Darling enthusiast, holy child,
Too good for this world's warring wild,
Too heavenly now but doomed to be
Hell-like in heart and misery.

And what shall change that angel brow
And quench that spirit's glorious glow?
Relentless laws that disallow
True virtue and true joy below.

And blame me not, if, when the dread
Of suffering clouds thy youthful head,
If when by crime and sorrow tost
Thy wandering bark is wrecked and lost

I too depart, I too decline,
And make thy path no longer mine.
'Tis thus that human minds will turn,
All doomed alike to sin and mourn
Yet all with long gaze fixed afar,
Adoring virtue's distant star.

The sentence of exile was more than Amedeus could bear. Bitterly he begged

For lifelong chains or timeless tomb
Or any but an Exile's doom.

Angelica added her pleadings to his, but to no effect, nor did the wretched two receive help or comfort from Lord Alfred, who, completely under Augusta's influence, joined her in driving them into a foreign land, where with other exiles, they entered upon a career of outlawry. This part of the story is told in "Written in Aspin Castle" and "The Death of A. G. A."

It may be that the two following unidentified poems record Angelica's sorrow under A. G. A.'s betrayal.

The inspiring music's thrilling sound,[14]
The glory of the festal day,
The glittering splendour rising round,
Have passed like all earth's joys away.

Forsaken by that Lady fair
She glides unheeding through them all
Covering her brow to hide the tear
That still, though checked, trembles to fall.

She hurries through the outer Hall
And up the stairs through galleries dim
That murmur to the breezes' call
The night-wind's lonely vesper hymn.

It is not pride, it is not shame,[15]
That makes her leave the gorgeous hall;
And though neglect her heart might tame
She mourns not for her sudden fall.

'Tis true she stands among the crowd
An unmarked and an unloved child,
While each young comrade, blithe and proud,
Glides through the maze of pleasure wild.

And all do homage to their will,
And all seem glad their voice to hear;
She heeds not that, but hardly still
Her eye can hold the quivering tear.

What made her weep, what made her glide
Out to the park this dreary day,
And cast her jewelled chains aside,
And seek a rough and lonely way,

[14] This poem is the last of the four pieces written on one side of a single
sheet, the second of which is dated July 12, 1836. (See chap. I, note 1.)
It has no identifying heading.

[15] The manuscript of this poem, on a torn scrap of paper, bears no date
or identifying heading.

And down beneath a cedar's shade
On the wet grass regardless lie,
With nothing but its gloomy head
Between her and the showery sky?

I saw her stand in the gallery long,
Watching the little children there,
As they were playing the pillars among
And bounding down the marble stair.

CHAPTER V

Julius Again

IN TIME Lord Alfred found his daughter's misery visited on his own head, for again Julius Brenzaida crossed Augusta's path. Piqued and tantalized by his cold and scornful attitude, she exerted all her charms to bring him to her feet. But Julius had learned his early lesson well and refused to put himself again in her power. Her vanity reacted upon herself to bring into being and to make her the slave of the one deep and lasting love of her life. Through month after month Julius called her at pleasure to love trysts upon the moors.

> Geraldine, the moon is shining[1]
> With so soft, so bright a ray;
> Seems it not that eve, declining,
> Ushered in a fairer day?

[1] The manuscripts of this and the next poem are each initialed "E." and dated October 17, 1838. They carry the identifying headings "Song by J. Brenzaida to G. S." [Song by Julius Brenzaida to Geraldine S.]. From other poems, as the story develops, it becomes evident that A. G. A. and Geraldine are one, i.e., A. G. A.'s middle initial stands for Geraldine, and thus for the first time we have the heroine's full name, Augusta Geraldine Almeda. Only once again is the middle name used, in a poem headed "Geraldine" (" 'Twas night; her comrades gathered all"), identifying her as the mother of Julius's child. As the wife of Lord Alfred S., she would be correctly designated as G. S.

While the wind is whispering only,
Far—across the water borne,
Let us in this silence lonely
Sit beneath the ancient thorn.

Wild the road, and rough and dreary;
Barren all the moorland round;
Rude the couch that rests us weary;
Mossy stone and heathy ground.

But, when winter storms were meeting
In the moonless, midnight dome,
Did we heed the tempest's beating,
Howling round our spirits' home?

No; that tree with branches riven,
Whitening in the whirl of snow,
As it tossed against the heaven,
Sheltered happy hearts below—

And at Autumn's mild returning
Shall our feet forget the way?
And in Cynthia's silver morning,
Geraldine, wilt thou delay?

At last, tiring of the intrigue, he demanded that she send Lord
Alfred away and acknowledge himself as her husband.[2] When
she demurred in noble speech, he asked scornfully wherein lay
the crime of saying good-by to Alfred, when she had long ago
betrayed him in her heart, adding that this was the last offer he
would make her. If she could forget her vows to him, he could
forget her charms in those of other women who had loved him
long and faithfully.

[2] The Young Men's Play and the Angrian stories treat of a completely
amoral society. Romantic love is the only recognized obligation between
husband and wife. Charlotte in one of her Angrian stories explained a
quick marriage-shift by remarking casually that in Angrian society di-
vorce was a matter quickly and easily arranged. Though Emily in her Gon-
dal poems never forgets the reality of sin and its consequences, she seems
to have carried over many of the customs and conventions of the Young
Men's Play. Certainly there is no evidence that Gondal society laid any
restrictions upon A. G. A.'s matrimonial impulses.

I knew not 'twas so dire a crime
To say the word, Adieu;
But this shall be the only time
My slighted heart shall sue.

The wild moorside, the winter morn,
The gnarled and ancient tree—
If in your breast they waken scorn,
Shall wake the same in me.

I can forget black eyes and brows,
And lips of rosy charm,
If you forget the sacred vows
Those faithless lips could form.

If hard commands can tame your love,
Or prison walls can hold,
I would not wish to grieve above
A thing so false and cold.

And there are bosoms bound to mine
With links both tried and strong;
And there are eyes whose lightning shine
Has warmed and blessed me long:

Those eyes shall make my only day,
Shall set my spirit free,
And chase the foolish thoughts away
That mourn your memory!

Julius's ultimatum brought Geraldine or A. G. A. to his terms, and she sent Lord Alfred away, acknowledging that she had wronged him, and yet, as always, justifying her action in poetic speech.

This summer wind, with thee and me[3]
Roams in the dawn of day;
But thou must be where it shall be,
Ere Evening—far away.

[3] The manuscript of this poem, initialed "E." and dated March 2, 1844, has the heading "A. G. A. to A. S." The close connection of the poem in plot development with the two foregoing seems to make it certain that Geraldine and A. G. A. are one.

The farewell's echo from thy soul
Should not depart before
Hills rise and distant rivers roll
Between us evermore.

I know that I have done thee wrong—
Have wronged both thee and Heaven—
And I may mourn my lifetime long
Yet may not be forgiven.

Repentant tears will vainly fall
To cancel deeds untrue;
But for no grief can I recall
The dreary word—Adieu.

Yet thou a future peace shalt win
Because thy soul is clear;
And I who had the heart to sin
Will find a heart to bear.

Till far beyond earth's frenzied strife
That makes destruction joy,
Thy perished faith shall spring to life
And my remorse shall die.

In sacrificing Lord Alfred to her love for Julius, A. G. A., in another version of the parting, represents herself as controlled by fate, taking no moral responsibility for her cruelty. She had loved Alfred as one loves the moon; who could blame her that his attractions faded in the brilliance of Julius's sunlike rays?

Yes, holy be thy resting place[4]
Wherever thou may'st lie;
The sweetest winds breathe on thy face,
The softest of the sky.

And will not guardian Angels send
Kind dreams and thoughts of love,

[4] This poem, itself undated, is written on a single loose sheet, the reverse of which bears the date July 26, 1843 (possibly 1842—the last figure is indistinct). There is no identifying heading, but the connection with the foregoing poem is made certain in the concluding stanza.

Though I no more may watchful bend
Thy longed repose above?

And will not heaven itself bestow
A beam of glory there
That summer's grass more green may grow,
And summer's flowers more fair?

Farewell, farewell, 'tis hard to part
Yet, loved one, it must be:
I would not rend another heart
Not even by blessing thee.

Go! we must break affection's chain,
Forget the hopes of years:
Nay, grieve not—willest thou remain
To waken wilder tears?

This wild breeze with thee and me
Roved in the dawning day;
And thou shouldest be where it shall be
Ere evening, far away.

Yet A. G. A. did not go unscathed by conscience—and the hurt
was enhanced by a gentle though persistent questioner, probably
Lord Eldred W.

"Thou standest in the greenwood now[5]
The place, the hour the same—[6]
And here the fresh leaves gleam and glow
And there, down in the lake below,
The tiny ripples flame.

"The breeze sings like a summer breeze
Should sing in summer skies
And tower-like rocks and tent-like trees
In mingled glory rise.

10 "But where is he to-day, to-day?"
"O question not with me."

[5] The manuscript of this undated poem initialed "E.," carries the identi-
fying heading "To A. G. A."
[6] The reference is to the love scene depicted in "At such a time in such a
spot," headed "A. G. A. to A. S." (See beginning of chap. IV.)

"I will not, Lady; only say
   Where may thy lover be?

"Is he upon some distant shore
   Or is he on the sea
   Or is the heart thou dost adore
   A faithless heart to thee?"

"The heart I love, what'er betide,
   Is faithful as the grave
20 And neither foreign lands divide
   Nor yet the rolling wave."

"Then why should sorrow cloud that brow
   And tears those eyes bedim?
   Reply this once—is it that thou
   Hast faithless been to him?"

"I gazed upon the cloudless moon
   And loved her all the night
   Till morning came and ardent noon,
   Then I forgot her light—

30 "No—not forgot—eternally
   Remains its memory dear;
   But could the day seem dark to me
   Because the night was fair?

"I well may mourn that only one
   Can light my future sky
   Even though by such a radiant sun
   My moon of life must die."[7]

In another poem, without heading but readily identified, A. G. A. expands and intensifies the figure of Julius as the sun of her life, paling into invisibility all other loves and loyalties.

Ah! why, because the dazzling sun[8]
   Restored my earth to joy
   Have you departed, every one,
   And left a desert sky?

[7] There is an earlier and incomplete draft of this poem beginning, "I'm standing in the forest now."

[8] The manuscript of this poem, dated April 14, 1845, has no identifying heading.

All through the night, your glorious eyes
Were gazing down in mine,
And with a full heart's thankful sighs
I blessed that watch divine!

I was at peace, and drank your beams
10 As they were life to me
And revelled in my changeful dreams
Like petrel on the sea.

Thought followed thought—star followed star
Through boundless regions on,
While one sweet influence, near and far,
Thrilled through and proved us one.

Why did the morning rise to break
So great, so pure a spell,
And scorch with fire the tranquil cheek
20 Where your cool radiance fell?

Blood-red he rose, and arrow-straight
His fierce beams struck my brow:
The soul of Nature sprang elate,
But mine sank sad and low!

My lids closed down—yet through their veil
I saw him blazing still;
And bathe in gold the misty dale,
And flash upon the hill.

I turned me to the pillow then
30 To call back Night, and see
Your worlds of solemn light, again
Throb with my heart and me!

It would not do—the pillow glowed
And glowed both roof and floor,
And birds sang loudly in the wood,
And fresh winds shook the door.

The curtains waved, the wakened flies
Were murmuring round my room,
Imprisoned there, till I should rise
40 And give them leave to roam.

O Stars and Dreams and Gentle Night;
O Night and Stars return!
And hide me from the hostile light
That does not warm, but burn—

That drains the blood of suffering men;
Drinks tears, instead of dew:
Let me sleep through his blinding reign,
And only wake with you!

Lord Alfred made his way to England and there died by his own hand. His spirit, thus shut out from heaven, "an outcast for eternity," returned to grieve around Aspin Castle.

How do I love on summer nights[9]
To sit within this Norman door,
Whose sombre portal hides the lights
Thickening above me evermore!

How do I love to hear the flow
Of Aspin's water murmuring low;
And hours long listen to the breeze
That sighs in Rockden's waving trees.

To-night, there is no wind to wake
10 One ripple on the lonely lake;
To-night, the clouds subdued and grey
Starlight and moonlight shut away.

'Tis calm and still and almost drear,
So utter is the solitude;
But still I love to linger here
And form my mood to nature's mood.

There's a wild walk beneath the rocks
Following the bend of Aspin's side;
'Tis worn by feet of mountain-flocks
20 That wander down to drink the tide.

[9] The manuscript of this poem, initialed "E.," has the two dates, August 20, 1842, and February 6, 1843, showing that it was begun in Brussels when Emily was studying in Pensionnat Héger and completed at Haworth after her return, being half a year in the writing. It bears the identifying heading "Written in Aspin Castle."

Never by cliff and gnarlèd tree
Wound fairy path so sweet to me;
Yet of the native shepherds none,
In open day and cheerful sun,
Will tread its labyrinths alone;
Far less when evening's pensive hour
Hushes the bird and shuts the flower,
And gives to Fancy magic power
O'er each familiar tone.

30 For round their hearths they'll tell the tale,
And every listener swears it true,
How wanders there a phantom pale
With spirit-eyes of dreamy blue.

It always walks with head declined,
Its long curls move not in the wind,
Its face is fair—divinely fair;
But brooding on that angel brow
Rests such a shade of deep despair
As nought divine could ever know.

40 How oft in twilight, lingering lone,
I've stood to watch that phantom rise,
And seen in mist and moonlit stone
Its gleaming hair and solemn eyes.

The ancient men, in secret, say
'Tis the first chief of Aspin grey
That haunts his feudal home;
But why, around that alien grave
Three thousand miles beyond the wave,
Where his exiled ashes lie
50 Under the cope of England's sky,
Doth he not rather roam?

I've seen his picture in the hall;
It hangs upon an eastern wall,
And often when the sun declines
That picture like an angel shines;
And when the moonbeam, chill and blue,
Streams the spectral windows through,
That picture's like a spectre too.

The hall is full of portraits rare;
60 Beauty and mystery mingle there:
At his right hand an infant fair
Looks from its golden frame;
And just like his its ringlets bright,
Its large dark eye of shadowy light,
Its cheeks' pure hue, its forehead white,
And like its noble name.

Daughter divine![10] and could his gaze
Fall coldly on thy peerless face?
And did he never smile to see
70 Himself restored to infancy?

Never part back that golden flow
Of curls, and kiss that pearly brow,
And feel no other earthly bliss
Was equal to that parent's kiss?

No; turn towards the western side:
There stands Sidonia's deity,[11]
In all her glory, all her pride!
And truly like a god she seems:
Some god of wild enthusiast's dreams;
80 And this is she for whom he died:
For whom his spirit, unforgiven,
Wanders unsheltered, shut from heaven—
An outcast for eternity.

Those eyes are dust, those lips are clay;
That form is mouldered all away;
Nor thought, nor sense, nor pulse, nor breath:
The whole devoured and lost in death!

There is no worm, however mean,
That, living, is not nobler now
90 Than she, Lord Alfred's idol queen,
So loved, so worshipped, long ago.[12]

[10] Her name, Angelica, is learned from "The Death of A. G. A.," line 29.
[11] See chap. IV, note 1.
[12] Compare this and the foregoing stanza with the last section of "The Death of A. G. A.," lines 329–332.

O come away! the Norman door
Is silvered with a sudden shine;
Come, leave these dreams o'er things of yore
And turn to Nature's face divine.

O'er wood and wold, o'er flood and fell,
O'er flashing lake and gleaming dell,
The harvest moon looks down;
And when heaven smiles with love and light,
100 And earth looks back so dazzling bright—
In such a scene, on such a night,
Earth's children should not frown.

CHAPTER VI

Conquest

UNDER ROSINA'S driving ambition, Prince Julius of Angora, in Gondal, who as one of the *conquistadores* of Gaaldine was also King of Almedore, set out to make himself sole ruler of both islands. First he attacked the Gaaldine branch of the Exina family, his strongest rival, besieging and taking the capital city, Zalona.

> All blue and bright, in glorious light,[1]
> The morn comes marching on;
> And now Zalona's steeples white
> Glow golden in the sun.
>
> This day might be a festal day:
> The streets are crowded all;
> And emerald flags stream broad and gay[2]
> From turret, tower, and wall.

[1] The manuscript of this poem, initialed "E. J." and dated February 24, 1843, has the heading "On the Fall of Zalona." It is one of Emily's several realistic pictures of war, written, no doubt, in protest against Charlotte's and Branwell's glorification of war. See Ratchford, "War in Gondal," *The Trollopian*, June, 1948, 73–78.

Closely related to this poem in subject and tone is an unidentified piece beginning "A sudden chasm of ghastly light," dated October 14, 1837 (see Hatfield, *Complete Poems*, p. 50), important in that it foreshadows Lockwood's nightmare in *Wuthering Heights*.

[2] The flag of the Exina family was green; Brenzaida's flag was red.

And, hark! how music evermore
10 Is sounding in the sky:
The deep bells boom, the cannon roar,
The trumpets sound on high—

The deep bells boom, the deep bells clash,
Upon the reeling air;
The cannon with unceasing crash
Make answer far and near.

What do those brazen tongues proclaim,
What joyous fête begun?
What offering to our country's fame,
20 What noble victory won?

Go, ask that solitary sire,
Laid in his house alone,
His silent hearth without a fire
His sons and daughters gone.

Go, ask those children in the street,
Beside their mother's door,
Waiting to hear the lingering feet
That they shall hear no more.

Ask those pale soldiers round the gates,
30 With famine-kindled eye:
They'll say, "Zalona celebrates
The day that she must die."

The charger, by his manger tied,
Has rested many a day;
Yet, ere the spur have touched his side,
Behold, he sinks away!

And hungry dogs, with wolf-like cry,
Unburied corpses tear,
While their gaunt masters gaze and sigh
40 And scarce the feast forbear.

Now, look down from Zalona's wall—
There war the unwearied foe;
If ranks before our cannon fall,
New ranks for ever grow.

And many a week, unbroken thus
Their troops our ramparts hem;
And for each man that fights for us,
A hundred fight for them!

Courage and Right and spotless Truth
50 Were pitched 'gainst trait'rous crime;
We offered all—our age, our youth,
Our brave men in their prime—

And all have failed—the fervent prayers;
The trust in heavenly aid;
Valour and Faith and sealèd tears
That would not mourn the dead;

Lips, that did breathe no murmuring word;
Hearts, that did ne'er complain,
Though vengeance held a sheathèd sword,
60 And martyrs bled in vain.

Alas, alas, the Myrtle bowers
By blighting blasts destroyed!
Alas, the Lily's withered flowers
That leave the garden void!

Unfolds o'er tower, and waves o'er height,
A sheet of crimson sheen:
Is it the setting sun's red light
That stains our standard green?

Heaven help us in this awful hour!
70 For now might Faith decay—
Now might we doubt God's guardian power
And curse instead of pray.

He will not even let us die—
Not let us die at home;
The foe must see our soldiers fly
As they had feared the tomb;

Because we *dare* not stay to gain
Those longed-for, glorious graves—
We dare not shrink from slavery's chain
80 To leave our children slaves!

But when this scene of awful woe
Has neared its final close,
As God forsook our armies, so
May He forsake our foes!

Insensible or indifferent to the misery and ruin he had brought
upon a proud and noble city, Julius gloried in his conquest and
prepared to invade Gondal.

Awake! awake! how loud the stormy morning[3]
Calls up to life the nations resting round;
Arise! arise! is it the voice of mourning
That breaks our slumber with so wild a sound?

The voice of mourning? Listen to its pealing;
That shout of triumph drowns the sigh of woe.
Each tortured heart forgets its wonted feeling;
Each faded cheek resumes its long-lost glow.

Our souls are full of gladness; God has given
Our arms to victory, our foes to death;
The crimson ensign waves its sheet in heaven,
The sea-green Standard lies in dust beneath.

Patriots, no stain is on your country's glory;
Soldiers, preserve that glory bright and free.
Let Almedore,[4] in peace, and battle gory,
Be still a nobler name for victory!

Warned of the stars, Lord Eldred pleaded in vain against the
campaign. In a dream he saw and heard omens of disaster.

The night of storms has passed,[5]
The sunshine bright and clear
Gives glory to the verdant waste
And warms the breezy air;

[3] The manuscript used here is not dated, but bears the identifying head-
ing "Song by Julius Angora" [Julius Brenzaida, Prince of Angora]. A can-
celed manuscript agreeing in text bears the date December, 1837, and
identification, "J. A."

[4] Julius of Angora, in Gondal, was also ruler of Almedore, in Gaaldine.

[5] This poem, signed "E. J. Brontë" and dated June 10, 1837, has no
identifying heading. The speaker is probably Lord Eldred. (See chap. IV,
note 6.)

And I would leave my bed,
Its cheering smile to see,
To chase the visions from my head
Whose forms have troubled me.

In all the hours of gloom
10 My soul was wrapt away;
I dreamt I stood by a marble tomb
Where royal corpses lay.

It was just the time of eve
When parted ghosts might come
Above their prisoned dust to grieve
And wail their woeful doom.

And truly at my side
I saw a shadowy thing
Most dim, and yet its presence there
20 Curdled my blood with ghastly fear
And ghastlier wondering.

My breath I could not draw,
The air seemed ranny;[6]
But still my eyes with maddening gaze
Were fixed upon its fearful face,
And its were fixed on me.

I fell down on the stone,
But could [not] turn away;
My words died in a voiceless moan
30 When I began to pray.

And still it bent above,
Its features full in view;
It seemed close by, and yet more far
Than this world from the farthest star
That tracks the boundless blue.

Indeed, 'twas not the space
Of earth or time between,

[6] This word is defined by Hatfield as "a north of England colloquialism,
meaning 'sharp' or 'keen.' "

But the sea of death's eternity,
The gulph o'er which mortality
40 Has never, never been.

O bring not back again
The horror of that hour
When its lips opened, and a sound
Awoke the stillness reigning round,
Faint as a dream, but the earth shrank
And heaven's lights shivered 'neath its power.

"Woe for the day; Regina's[7] pride,
Regina's hope is in the grave;
And who shall rule my land beside,
50 And who shall save?

"Woe for the day; with gory tears
My country's sons this day shall rue.
Woe for the day; a thousand years
Can not repair what one shall do.

"Woe for the day." Mixt with the wind,
That sad lament was ringing;
It almost broke my heart to hear
Such dreary, dreary singing.

Neither moral force nor fear could deter the ambitious Rosina
and the conquest-mad Julius. The expedition left Gaaldine with
the crimson flag of the Brenzaida family waving from every mast,
while bands on deck played triumphant martial music. Julius's
Gaaldine forces joined with his army in Angora to effect a swift
victory. Gerald Exina, King of Gondal, weakened by the family's
defeat in Zalona and unable to repel the invaders, allowed Julius
to be crowned as joint sovereign with himself in the great na-
tional cathedral in Regina, the capital city of Gondal.

[7] Regina was the capital of Gondal and the seat of Julius's imperial gov-
ernment. (See Introduction, p. 19.) In the first stanza of Anne's "An Or-
phan's Lament" we read:

> . . . twice the summer's sun
> Has gilt Regina's towers,
> And melted wild Angora's snows,
> And warmed Exina's bowers.

The wide cathedral aisles are lone,[8]
The vast crowds vanished, every one;
There can be nought beneath that dome
But the cold tenants of the tomb.

O look again, for still on high
The lamps are burning gloriously;
And look again, for still beneath
A thousand thousand live and breathe.

All mute as death regard the shrine
That gleams in lustre so divine,
Where Gondal's monarchs, bending low
After the hush of silent prayer,
Take, in heaven's sight, their awful vow,
And never dying union swear.
King Julius lifts his impious eye
From the dark marble to the sky;
Blasts with that Oath his perjured soul,
And changeless is his cheek the while,
Though burning thoughts, that spurn control,
Kindle a short and bitter smile,
As face to face the kinsmen stand,
His false hand clasped in Gerald's hand.

To Julius the joint coronation was but the first step in making
himself sole ruler of Gondal. Accusing Gerald of unfaithfulness
to his oath, he threw him into prison to die.

His land may burst the galling chain,[9]
His people may be free again,
For them a thousand hopes remain,
But hope is dead for him.
Soft falls the moonlight on the sea
Whose wild waves play at liberty,
And Gondal's wind sings solemnly
Its native midnight hymn.

[8] The manuscript of this poem, dated March, 1838, has no identifying
heading, nor needs any, for it tells its own story. It is written on the reverse
of the undated sheet referred to in chap. III, note 15.
[9] The manuscript of this poem has neither date nor heading, but its place
in the narrative is plain.

Around his prison walls it sings,
His heart is stirred through all its strings,
Because that sound remembrance brings
Of scenes that once have been.
His soul has left the storm below,
And reached a realm of sunless snow;
The region of unchanging woe,
Made voiceless by despair.

And Gerald's land may burst its chain,
His subjects may be free again;
For them a thousand hopes remain,
But hope is dead for him.
Set is his sun of liberty;
Fixed is his earthly destiny;
A few years of captivity,
And then a captive's tomb.

CHAPTER VII

Revenge

ESTABLISHED as emperor of Gondal, Julius believed his conquest complete. The Exina family and their adherents were dead, imprisoned, or in exile. Other Gondal princes hastened to swear allegiance to Julius, while even foreign rulers trembled for their thrones. But the country was far from acquiescing in the new order. Patriots allied themselves with outlaws in a plot to assassinate the usurper. In their secret cavern stronghold the plotters, led by Angelica, who saw her opportunity for revenge upon A. G. A. through Julius, bound themselves by oath to the deed, perfected their plans, and cast lots for the parts they should play.[1] Apparently the lot of actual assassin fell upon Amedeus.

> The day is done, the winter sun[2]
> Is setting in its sullen sky;
> And drear the course that has been run,
> And dim the beams that slowly die.
>
> No star will light my coming night;
> No moon of hope for me will shine;

[1] "The Death of A. G. A.," line 101 ff.

[2] The manuscript of this poem is headed "A. S. Castle Wood," and dated February 2, 1844. The speaker is quite certainly Amedeus, the dark boy of sorrow. Both the situation and the initials A. S. indicate that he is speaking to Angelica, the daughter of Lord Alfred of Aspin Castle. "Castle Wood" is probably the name of the outlaws' stronghold.

I mourn not heaven would blast my sight,
And I never longed for ways divine.

Through Life hard Task I did not ask
Celestial aid, celestial cheer;
I saw my fate without its mask,
And met it too without a tear.

The grief that prest this living breast
Was heavier far than earth can be;
And who would dread eternal rest
When labour's hire was agony?

Dark falls the fear of this despair
On spirits born for happiness;
But I was bred the mate of care,
The foster-child of sore distress.

No sighs for me, no sympathy,
No wish to keep my soul below;
The heart is dead since infancy,
Unwept-for let the body go.

Cast in a traitor's role, M. Douglas, one of the conspirators, found his part hard to play, fearing most of all the abhorrence of his sweetheart, E. R. Gleneden, a member of the Exina family.

The moon is full this winter night;[8]
The stars are clear though few;
And every window glistens bright
With leaves of frozen dew.

The sweet moon through your lattice gleams
And lights your room like day;
And there you pass in happy dreams
The peaceful hours away;

While I, with effort hardly quelling
10 The anguish in my breast,
Wander about the silent dwelling
And cannot think of rest.

[8] The manuscript of this poem, dated November 21, 1844, is headed "M. Douglas to E. R. Gleneden." The relation of M. Douglas to Douglas of "The Death of A. G. A." is not clear.

The old clock in the gloomy hall
Ticks on from hour to hour,
And every time its measured call
Seems lingering slow and slower.

And O how slow that keen-eyed star
Has tracked the chilly grey!
What watching yet, how very far
20 The morning lies away!

Beside your chamber door I stand:
Love, are you slumbering still?
My cold heart underneath my hand
Has almost ceased to thrill.

Bleak, bleak the east wind sobs and sighs
And drowns the turret bell
Whose sad note, undistinguished, dies
Unheard, like my farewell.

To-morrow Scorn will blight my name
30 And Hate will trample me—
Will load me with a coward's shame:
A Traitor's perjury!

False Friends will launch their venomed sneers;
True Friends will wish me dead;
And I shall cause the bitterest tears
That you have ever shed.

The dark deeds of my outlawed race
Will then like virtues shine;
And men will pardon their disgrace,
40 Beside the guilt of mine;

For who forgives the accursed crime
Of dastard treachery?
Rebellion in its chosen time
May Freedom's champion be;

Revenge may stain a righteous sword,
It may be just to slay;
But, Traitor—Traitor—from that word
All true breasts shrink away!

O I would give my heart to death,
50   To keep my honour fair:
    Yet, I'll not give my inward Faith
    My Honour's name to spare—

Not even to keep your priceless love,
  Dare I, Beloved, deceive;
This treason should the future prove:
  Gleneden, then believe!

I know the path I ought to go;
  I follow fearlessly,
Enquiring not what deeper woe
60   Stern Duty stores for me.

So Foes pursue, and cold allies
  Mistrust me, every one:
Let me be false in others' eyes
  If faithful in my own.

It may be that a brother of E. R. Gleneden and his sweetheart were also involved in the plot.

Thy Guardians are asleep,[4]
  So I've come to bid thee rise:
Thou hast a holy vow to keep
  Ere yon crescent quit the skies.

Though clouds careering wide
  Will hardly let her gleam,
She's bright enough to be our guide
  Across the mountain-stream.

O waken, Dearest, wake!
  What means this long delay?
Say, wilt thou not for honour's sake
  Chase idle fears away?

Think not of future grief
  Entailed on present joy:

[4] The manuscript of this poem, initialed "E." and dated May 4, 1843, has the heading "E. G. to M. R." The text explains these initials as E. Gleneden and Mary R.

An age of woe were only brief
Its memory to destroy.

And neither Hell nor Heaven,
Though both conspire at last,
Can take the bliss that has been given,
Can rob us of the past.

Then, waken, Mary, wake:
How canst thou linger now?
For true love's and Gleneden's sake,
Arise and keep thy vow.

The plot succeeded perfectly.

King Julius left the south country[5]
His banners all bravely flying;
His followers went out with Jubilee
But they shall return with sighing.

Loud arose the triumphal hymn
The drums were loudly rolling,
Yet you might have heard in distance dim
How a passing bell was tolling.

The sword so bright from battles won
With unseen rust is fretting,
The evening comes before the noon,
The scarce risen sun is setting.

While princes hang upon his breath
And nations round are fearing,
Close by his side a daggered death
With sheathless point stands sneering.

That death he took a certain aim,
For Death is stony-hearted
And in the zenith of his fame
Both power and life departed.

Amedeus, who struck the fatal blow, was in turn struck down

[5] The manuscript, dated April 20, 1839, is headed merely "Song."

by the Emperor's guards;[6] Douglas made his escape.[7] In the meantime, a member of the Gleneden family, probably Arthur, buried like Gerald in a dungeon, dreams that his was the privilege of saving Gondal by stabbing Julius.

> Tell me, watcher, is it winter?[8]
> Say how long my sleep has been?
> Have the woods I left so lovely
> Lost their robes of tender green?
>
> Is the morning slow in coming?
> Is the night-time loath to go?
> Tell me, are the dreary mountains
> Drearier still with drifted snow?
>
> "Captive, since thou sawest the forest,
> 10 All its leaves have died away,
> And another March has woven
> Garlands for another May.
>
> "Ice has barred the Arctic water,
> Soft south winds have set it free;
> And once more to deep green valley
> Golden flowers might welcome thee."
>
> Watcher, in this lonely prison,
> Shut from joy and kindly air,
> Heaven, descending in a vision,
> 20 Taught my soul to do and bear.
>
> It was night, a night in winter;
> I lay on the dungeon floor,
> And all other sounds were silent—
> All, except the river's roar.
>
> Over Death and Desolation,
> Fireless hearths and lifeless homes;

6 "Rosina" ("Weeks of wild delirium past") and "The Death of A. G. A."
7 Possibly M. Douglas (above), but more likely a kinsman who appears in "The Death of A. G. A."
8 The manuscript of this poem, initialed "E." and dated May 21, 1838, is headed "Gleneden's Dream." Gleneden is probably Arthur, lamented by his sister in "From our evening fireside now."

Over orphans' heart-sick sorrows,
Over fathers' bloody tombs;

Over friends, that my arms never
30 Might embrace in love again—
Memory pondered, until madness
Struck its poignard in my brain.

Deepest slumber followed raving,
Yet, methought, I brooded still;
Still I saw my country bleeding,
Dying for a Tyrant's will—

Not because *my* bliss was blasted,
Burned within, the avenging flame;
Not because my scattered kindred
40 Died in woe or lived in shame.

God doth know, I would have given
Every bosom dear to me,
Could that sacrifice have purchased
Tortured Gondal's liberty!

But, that at Ambition's bidding
All her cherished hopes should wane;
That her noblest sons should muster,
Strive and fight, and fall in vain—

Hut and castle, hall and cottage,
50 Roofless, crumbling to the ground—
Mighty Heaven, a glad Avenger
Thy eternal justice found!

Yes, the arm that once would shudder
Even to pierce a wounded deer,
I beheld it, unrelenting,
Choke in blood it's sovereign's prayer.

Glorious dream! I saw the city
Blazing in imperial shine;
And among adoring thousands
60 Stood a man of form divine.

None need point the princely victim—
Now he smiles with royal pride!
Now his glance is bright as lightning;
Now—the knife is in his side!

Ha, I saw how death could darken—
Darken that triumphant eye!
His red heart's blood drenched my dagger;
My ear drank his dying sigh!

Shadows come! What means this midnight?
70 Oh my God, I know it all!
Know the fever-dream is over!
Unavenged the Avengers fall!

In dungeons dark I cannot sing,[9]
In sorrow's thrall 'tis hard to smile:
What bird can soar with broken wing,
What heart can bleed and joy the while?

Just before or following close upon Julius's coronation, A. G. A., here again called Rosina, had fallen desperately ill. Upon regaining consciousness after weeks of delirium, she read evil tidings in the faces of her waiting ladies and forced them to tell her the truth—that Brenzaida's empire was overthrown.

Weeks of wild delirium past,[10]
Weeks of fevered pain;
Rest from suffering comes at last;
Reason dawns again.[11]

[9] This poem is the first of a group of four pieces on one side of a manuscript sheet bearing the single date, September 23, 1838, the reverse of which carries four more poems. In the upper right-hand margin is written "Arthr Ex to ——" (apparently an abbreviated form of Arthur Exina), and underneath the dash is penciled the name "Marcius." Since Exina seems to be the territorial designation of the Gleneden family, the stanza is probably another prison plaint of Arthur Gleneden.

[10] The manuscript of this poem, dated September 1, 1841, bears the title "Rosina."

[11] Compare Cathy's illness in *Wuthering Heights*. The parallel suggests that the child of the poem headed "Geraldine" (" 'Twas night; her comrades gathered all") was born at this time.

It was a pleasant April day
Declining to the afternoon;
Sunshine upon her pillow lay
As warm as middle June.

It told her how unconsciously
10 Early spring had hurried by;
"Ah! Time has not delayed for me,"
She murmured with a sigh.

"Angora's hills have heard their tread;
The crimson flag is planted there;
Elderno's waves are rolling red,
While *I* lie fettered here.

"Nay; rather, Gondal's shaken throne
Is now secure and free;
And my King Julius reigns alone,
20 Debtless, alas! to me."

Loud was the sudden gush of woe
From those who watched around;
Rosina turned, and sought to know
Why burst that boding sound.

"What then, my dreams are false?" she said;
"Come, maidens, answer me:
Has Almedore in battle bled?[12]
Have slaves subdued the free?

"I know it all: he could not bear
30 To leave me dying far away;
He fondly, madly lingered here
And we have lost the day!

"But check those coward sobs, and bring
My robes, and smoothe my tangled hair:
A noble victory you shall sing
For every hour's despair!

[12] It will be noticed that Julius is here called by four names and titles—
King Julius, Angora (indicated), Almedore, and Brenzaida.

"When will he come? 'Twill soon be night:
He'll come when evening falls;
Oh, I shall weary for the light,
40 To leave my lonely halls!"

She turned her pallid face aside,
As she would seek repose;
But dark Ambition's thwarted pride
Forbade her lids to close.

And still on all who waited by
Oppressive mystery hung;
And swollen with grief was every eye,
And chained was every tongue.

They whispered nought but, "Lady, sleep;
50 Dear Lady, slumber now!
Had we not bitter cause to weep
While you were laid so low?

"And Hope can hardly deck the cheek
With sudden signs of cheer,
When it has worn through many a week
The stamp of anguish drear."

Fierce grew Rosina's gloomy gaze;
She cried, "Dissemblers, own,
Exina's arms in victory blaze;
60 Brenzaida's crest is down?"

"Well, since it must be told, Lady,
Brenzaida's crest *is* down;
Brenzaida's sun is set, Lady,
His empire overthrown!

"He died beneath this palace dome—
True hearts on every side;
Among his guards, within his home
Our glorious Monarch died.

"I saw him fall, I saw the gore
70 From his heart's fountain swell,
And mingling on the marble floor
His murderer's life-blood fell.

> And now, 'mid northern mountains lone,
> His desert grave is made;[13]
> And, Lady, of your love alone
> Remains a mortal shade!"

Julius's death was the severest blow of Rosina's tempestuous career. All of her strong ambition and imperious will, as well as her burning passion, centered in him. Earlier griefs—in her figurative speech—but plucked the blossoms and stripped the leaves from Time's branch, all to be restored "with ten-fold increase blessing" in Julius's love. Even sin was scared to distance by the glory of that love. His death severed her very life from its root.

> Death, that struck when I was most confiding[14]
> In my certain Faith of Joy to be,
> Strike again, Time's withered branch dividing
> From the fresh root of Eternity!
>
> Leaves, upon Time's branch, were growing brightly,
> Full of sap and full of silver dew;
> Birds, beneath its shelter, gathered nightly;
> Daily, round its flowers, the wild bees flew.
>
> Sorrow passed and plucked the golden blossom,
> 10 Guilt stripped off the foliage in its pride;
> But, within its parent's kindly bosom,
> Flowed forever Life's restoring tide.

[13] Compare this line with "Cold in the earth," second stanza, and "The organ swells," third and fourth stanzas, and note how each seems to contradict the other two as to Julius's burial place.

[14] The manuscript of this poem, dated April 10, 1845, has no heading, but A. G. A.'s familiar voice summarizing in poetic figures her own dramatic career identifies it as her cry of grief for Julius, in freshness of bereavement. In date of composition it follows immediately after "Cold in the earth" (March 3, 1845), and it was evidently written to emphasize how A. G. A.'s ambition and will to happiness triumphed over her natural affections, even her passion for Julius. It is significant that while Emily, naturally enough, entered "Cold in the earth," with its place name and personal heading, in her notebook marked "Gondal Poems," this companion piece, "Death, that struck," with no betraying marks of Gondal, went into her untitled notebook. She herself contributed the latter poem, with a few small changes, to *Poems*, 1846.

Little mourned I for the parted Gladness,
For the vacant nest and silent song;
Hope was there and laughed me out of sadness,
Whispering, "Winter will not linger long."

And behold, with tenfold increase blessing
Spring adorned the beauty-burdened spray;
Wind and rain and fervent heat caressing
20 Lavished glory on its second May.

High it rose; no wingèd grief could sweep it;
Sin was scared to distance with its shine:
Love and its own life had power to keep it
From all wrong, from every blight but thine!

Heartless Death, the young leaves droop and languish!
Evening's gentle air may still restore—
No: the morning sunshine mocks my anguish—
Time for me must never blossom more!

Strike it down, that other boughs may flourish
30 Where that perished sapling used to be;
Thus, at least, its mouldering corpse will nourish
That from which it sprung—Eternity.

CHAPTER VIII

Crumbling of an Empire

JULIUS'S DEATH signaled the overthrow of his empire and the restoration of the Exina dynasty, whose exiled and imprisoned adherents returned to their homes in joy subdued by grief for those who had fallen in the strife. The sorrow of that return is told by R. Gleneden, who finds home empty without her brother Arthur.

> From our evening fireside now,[1]
> Merry laugh and cheerful tone,
> Smiling eye and cloudless brow,
> Mirth and music, all are flown;
>
> Yet the grass before the door
> Grows as green in April rain;
> And as blithely as of yore
> Larks have poured their day-long strain.
>
> Is it fear or is it sorrow
> 10 Checks the stagnant stream of joy?
> Do we tremble that to-morrow
> May our present peace destroy?

[1] The manuscript of this poem, dated April 17, 1839, and initialed "E." is headed "By R. Gleneden." The speaker is probably E. R. Gleneden, Douglas's sweetheart, whom he addresses in "The moon is full this winter night," and the brother she mourns is Arthur Gleneden, the prisoner of "Gleneden's Dream" ("Tell me, watcher, is it winter?").

For past misery are we weeping?
What is past can hurt no more;
And the gracious heavens are keeping
Aid for that which lies before.

One is absent, and for one
Cheerless, chill is our hearthstone.
One is absent, and for him
20 Cheeks are pale and eyes are dim.

Arthur, brother, Gondal's shore
Rested from the battle's roar—
Arthur, brother, we returned
Back to Desmond lost and mourned.

Thou didst purchase by thy fall
Home for us and peace for all;
Yet, how darkly dawned that day—
Dreadful was the price to pay!

Just as once, through sun and mist
30 I have climbed the mountain's breast,
Still my gun, with certain aim,
Brought to earth the fluttering game;

But the very dogs repined;
Though I called with whistle shrill,
Listlessly they lagged behind,
Looking backward o'er the hill.

Sorrow was not vocal there:
Mute their pain and my despair;
But the joy of life was flown:
40 He was gone and we were lone.

So it is by morn and eve—
So it is in field and hall:
For the absent one we grieve,
One being absent saddens All.

R. Gleneden pictures also a group of young Gondalan nobles
returning to the Palace of Instruction in Gaaldine after a long
sojourn in Gondal.

Companions, all day long we've stood,[2]
The wild winds restless blowing;
All day we've watched the darkened flood
Around our vessel flowing.

Sunshine has never smiled since morn,
And clouds have gathered drear,
And heavier hearts would feel forlorn
And weaker minds would fear.

But look in each young shipmate's eyes
10   Lit by the evening flame,
And see how little stormy skies
Our joyous blood can tame.

No glance the same expression wears,
No lip the same soft smile;
Yet kindness warms and courage cheers:
Nerves every breast the while.

It is the hour of dreaming now,
The red fire brightly gleams;
And sweetest in a red fire's glow
20   The hour of dreaming seems.

I may not trace the thoughts of all,
But some I read as well
As I can hear the ocean's fall
And sullen surging swell.

Edmund's swift soul is gone before:
It threads a forest wide,
Whose towers are bending to the shore
And gazing on the tide.

And one is there; I know the voice,
30   The thrilling, stirring tone
That makes his bounding pulse rejoice,
Yet makes not *his* alone.

[2] The manuscript of this poem, initialed "E. J. B." and dated September
17, 1840, carries the name "R. Gleneden." It has no evident direct relation
to A. G. A., but its connection with the Gondal story is clear.

Mine own hand longs to clasp her hand,
Mine eye to greet her eye;
Win, white sails, win Zedora's strand
And Ula's Eden sky.

Mary and Flora, oft their gaze
Is clouded pensively,
And what that earnest aspect says
40 Is all revealed to me.

'Tis but two years, or little more,
Since first they dared that main;
And such a night may well restore
That first time back again.

The smothered sigh, the lingering late,
The longed-for, dreaded hour,
The parting at the moss-grown gate,
The last look on the tower:

I know they think of these, and then
50 The evening's gathering gloom,
And they alone, with foreign men
To guard their cabin room.

Mary Gleneden gives a picture of the reverse voyage—from Gaaldine to Gondal.

'Twas yesterday, at early dawn,[3]
I watched the falling snow;
A drearier scene on winter morn
Was never stretched below.

I could not see the mountains round,
But I knew by the wild wind's roar
How every drift, in their glens profound,
Was deepening ever more.

[3] The manuscript of this poem, dated December 19, 1843, is headed "M. G. for the U. S." [Mary Gleneden for the Unique Society]. The poem is unplaced in pattern, but evidently belongs to this series. Perhaps it was on this voyage that the Unique Society was wrecked, as Anne records in her birthday note of July 31, 1845. (See Appendix II.)

And then I thought of Ula's bowers
10 Beyond the southern sea;
Her tropic prairies bright with flowers
And rivers wandering free.

I thought of many a happy day
Spent in her Eden isle,
With my dear comrades, young and gay,
All scattered now so far away,
But not forgot the while!

Who that has breathed that heavenly air,
To northern climes would come,
20 To Gondal's mists and moorlands drear,
And sleet and frozen gloom?

Spring brings the swallow and the lark:
But what will winter bring?
Its twilight noons and evenings dark
To match the gifts of spring?

No! Look with me o'er that sullen main:
If thy spirit's eye can see,
There are brave ships floating back again
That no calm southern port could chain
30 From Gondal's stormy sea.

O how the hearts of the voyagers beat
To feel the frost-wind blow!
What flower in Ula's gardens sweet
Is worth one flake of snow?

The blast which almost rends their sail
Is welcome as a friend;
It brings them home, that thundering gale,
Home to their journey's end;

Home to our souls whose wearying sighs
40 Lament their absence drear,
And feel how bright even winter skies
Would shine if they were here!

The young nobles of Gondal, returning to the Palace of Instruction in Gaaldine, miss their fallen comrades, who had been the "life and soul" of the resistance to Julius's tyranny.

The busy day has hurried by,[4]
And hearts greet kindred hearts once more;
And swift the evening hours should fly,
But—what turns every gleaming eye
So often to the door,

And then so quick away—and why
Does sudden silence chill the room,
And laughter sink into a sigh,
And merry words to whispers die,
10 And gladness change to gloom?

O we are listening for a sound
We know shall ne'er be heard again;
Sweet voices in the halls resound,
Fair forms, fond faces gather round,
But all in vain—in vain!

Their feet shall never waken more
The echoes in these galleries wide,
Nor dare the snow on the mountain's brow,
Nor skim the river's frozen flow,
20 Nor wander down its side.

They who have been our life—our soul—
Through summer-youth, from childhood's spring—
Who bound us in one vigorous whole
To stand 'gainst Tyranny's control
For ever triumphing—

Who bore the brunt of battle's fray:
The first to fight, the last to fall;
Whose mighty minds, with kindred ray,
Still led the van in Glory's way;
30 The idol chiefs of all—

[4] The manuscript of this poem, initialed "E. J." and dated June 14, 1839, is headed "Written on Returning to the P. of I. [Palace of Instruction] on the 10th of January, 1827," but the speaker is not named. "January, 1827" is one of the four dates of Gondal chronology found in Emily's headings.

They, they are gone! Not for a while
As golden suns at night decline
And even in death our grief beguile
Foretelling, with a rose-red smile,
How bright the morn will shine.

No; these dark towers are lone and lorn;
This very crowd is vacancy;
And we must watch and wait and mourn
And half look out for their return,
40 And think their forms we see;

And fancy music in our ear,
Such as their lips could only pour;
And think we feel their presence near,
And start to find they are not here,
And never shall be more!

CHAPTER IX

The Fugitive

WITH THE OVERTHROW of Julius's empire, Rosina, or A. G. A., here again called Geraldine, became a fugitive with her infant daughter,[1] Alexandria, attended only by Lord Eldred. In hiding, in a rocky cave outside the city of Zedora in Gaaldine, she found joy in her child's resemblance to Julius. But even at this moment of peculiar tenderness, ambition rose above normal human feeling, to turn her "prayer" into poetic justification for ridding herself of the hampering care of the little one.

> 'Twas night; her comrades gathered all[2]
> Within their city's rocky wall;
> When flowers were closed and day was o'er,
> Their joyous hearts awoke the more.

[1] That the lovely lyric "Song to A. A." ("This shall be thy lullaby"—see Hatfield, *The Complete Poems* [1941], p. 71) records an incident in A. G. A.'s flight with her daughter is suggested by the story pattern and the initials of its heading. But a second draft of the poem signed "Blanche" injects an element of doubt, for there is no evidence that A. G. A. was known by that name.

[2] The manuscript of this poem, initialed "E." and dated August 17, 1841, bears the title "Geraldine," which is A. G. A.'s middle name. It is interesting and, perhaps, significant that this name is used alone but three times in Emily's Gondal poems—when A. G. A. is meeting Julius surreptitiously and when she is a fugitive following his death. (See chap. V, note 1.) "Geraldine" is Emily's parallel to Charlotte's long narrative poem depicting Zamorna in defeat and temporary exile from his throne.

But, lonely in her distant cave,
She heard the river's restless wave
Chafing its banks with dreamy flow:
Music for mirth and wail for woe.

Palm-trees and cedars towering high
10 Deepened the gloom of evening's sky;
And thick did raven ringlets veil
Her forehead, drooped like lily pale.

Yet I could hear my lady sing:
I knew she did not mourn;
For never yet from sorrow's spring
Such witching notes were born.

Thus poured she in that cavern wild
The voice of feeling warm,
As, bending o'er her beauteous child,
20 She clasped its sleeping form—

"Why sank so soon the summer sun
From our Zedora's skies?
I was not tired, my darling one,
Of gazing in thine eyes.

"Methought the heaven, whence thou hast come,
Was lingering there awhile;
And Earth seemed such an alien home
They did not dare to smile.

"Methought each moment something strange
30 Within their circles shone,
And yet, through every magic change,
They were Brenzaida's own.

"Methought—what thought I not, sweet love?
My whole heart centred there:
I breathed not but to send above
One gush of ardent prayer—

" 'Bless it, my gracious God,' I cried;
'Preserve thy mortal shrine;
For thine own sake, be thou its guide,
40 And keep it still divine!

" 'Say, sin shall never blanch that cheek,
Nor suffering charge[3] that brow;
Speak, in thy mercy, Maker, speak,
And seal it safe from woe!'

"Why did I doubt? In God's control[4]
Our mutual fates remain;
And pure as now my angel's soul
Must go to Heaven again."

The revellers in the city slept;
50 My lady, in her woodland bed;
I, watching o'er her slumber, wept
As one who mourns the dead!

The child's life was brief, even as Lord Eldred foresaw. A. G. A., having formed a resolve to return her "to Heaven again," carried it out relentlessly, but not without a struggle with her natural feelings.

Upon her soothing breast[5]
She lulled her little child;
A winter sunset in the west,
A dreary glory smiled.

For the exposure spot she chose a familiar and dearly loved mountain dell, where in summer she might have left her baby as in God's arms. But it was winter now; a mountain storm was raging, and "coldly spread the couch of snow."

[3] Hatfield's reading. Emily's *r*'s and *n*'s in this manuscript are so nearly identical that this word might justifiably be read *change*.

[4] Gradually and very reluctantly, the present editor came to the conviction that these two concluding stanzas pointing towards the child's death register A. G. A.'s resolution to commit infanticide. The specious reasoning and poetic speech are typically hers. Evidently such is the understanding of the speaker, pretty certainly Lord Eldred, who knew A. G. A.'s mind better than any other.

[5] This vignette, undated and without heading, together with an unfinished second poem, is written on a fragment of a sheet once joined to another fragment containing a poem dated December 19, 1839.

122]

I've seen this dell in July's shine[6]
As lovely as an angel's dream;
Above, heaven's depth of blue divine;
Around, the evening's golden beam.

I've seen the purple heather-bell
Look out by many a storm-worn stone;
And oh, I've seen such music swell,
Such wild notes wake these passes lone—

So soft, yet so intensely felt,
10   So low, yet so distinctly heard,
My breath would pause, my eyes would melt,
And my tears dew the green heath-sward.

I'd linger here a summer day,
Nor care how fast the hours flew by,
Nor mark the sun's departing ray
Smile sadly glorious from the sky.

Then, then I might have laid thee down
And deemed thy sleep would gentle be;
I might have left thee, darling one,
20   And thought thy God was guarding thee!

But now there is no wandering glow,
No gleam to say that God is nigh;
And coldly spreads thy couch of snow,
And harshly sounds thy lullaby.

Forests of heather, dark and long,
Wave their brown, branching arms above,
And they must soothe thee with their song,
And they must shield my child of love!

Alas, the flakes are heavily falling;
30   They cover fast each guardian crest;
And chilly white their shroud is palling
Thy frozen limbs and freezing breast.

[6] The manuscript of this poem, dated July 12, 1839, has the title "A Farewell to Alexandria."

Wakes up the storm more madly wild,
The mountain drifts are tossed on high—
Farewell, unblessed, unfriended child,
I cannot bear to watch thee die!

After a farewell embrace, A. G. A. laid the little one down beneath the brown waving branches of "forests of heather," and, with characteristic avoidance of painful experiences, would have hurried away, but her feet bound her to the spot.

The night is darkening round me,[7]
The wild winds coldly blow;
But a tyrant spell has bound me
And I cannot, cannot go.

The giant trees are bending
Their bare boughs weighed with snow,
And the storm is fast descending
And yet I cannot go.

Clouds beyond clouds above me,
Wastes beyond wastes below;
But nothing drear can move me;
I will not, cannot go.

[7] This poem, dated November, 1837, has no heading. It is followed on the same manuscript sheet by the sixteen-line poem, without heading, prophesying haunting remorse, "I'll come when thou art saddest."

CHAPTER X

Fifteen Wild Decembers

FORTUNE turned again for Augusta. Restored to her throne, she was crowned in the cathedral where Julius lay buried.[1]

> The organ swells, the trumpets sound,[2]
> The lamps in triumph glow;
> And none of all those thousands round
> Regards who sleeps below.
>
> Those haughty eyes that tears should fill
> Glance clearly, cloudlessly;
> Those bounding breasts, that grief should thrill,
> From thought of grief are free.
>
> His subjects and his soldiers there
> They blessed his rising bloom,
> But none a single sigh can spare
> To breathe above his tomb.
>
> Comrades in arms, I've looked to mark
> One shade of feeling swell,
> As your feet trod above the dark
> Recesses of his cell.

[1] See chap. VII, note 13.

[2] The manuscript of this poem, dated September 30, 1837, has no identifying heading. The text itself suggests its place in the story. The speaker is probably Lord Eldred.

To the world and even to those closest to A. G. A., it seemed that she, too, in the years that followed, had forgotten Julius. Yet fifteen years after his death, she pours out her grief for him in the most passionate and most convincing of her many avowals of eternal love.

> Cold in the earth, and the deep snow piled above thee![3]
> Far, far removed, cold in the dreary grave!
> Have I forgot, my Only Love, to love thee,
> Severed at last by Time's all-wearing wave?
>
> Now, when alone, do my thoughts no longer hover
> Over the mountains on Angora's shore;
> Resting their wings where heath and fern-leaves cover
> That noble heart for ever, ever more?
>
> Cold in the earth, and fifteen wild Decembers
> 10 From those brown hills have melted into spring—
> Faithful indeed is the spirit that remembers
> After such years of change and suffering!
>
> Sweet Love of youth, forgive if I forget thee
> While the World's tide is bearing me along:
> Sterner desires and darker hopes beset me,
> Hopes which obscure but cannot do thee wrong.
>
> No other Sun has lightened up my heaven;
> No other Star has ever shone for me:
> All my life's bliss from thy dear life was given—
> 20 All my life's bliss is in the grave with thee.
>
> But when the days of golden dreams had perished
> And even Despair was powerless to destroy,
> Then did I learn how existence could be cherished,
> Strengthened and fed without the aid of joy;
>
> Then did I check the tears of useless passion,
> Weaned my young soul from yearning after thine;

[3] The manuscript of this poem, dated March 3, 1845, carries the heading "R. Alcona to J. Brenzaida" [Rosina Alcona to Julius Brenzaida]. Its mood and sentiments, repeated in A. G. A.'s weariness of life, as expressed in "The Death of A. G. A." constitute one of the many evidences that Rosina and A. G. A. are one. In order of composition it immediately precedes "Death that struck when I was most confiding."

Sternly denied its burning wish to hasten
Down to that tomb already more than mine!

And even yet, I dare not let it languish,
30 Dare not indulge in Memory's rapturous pain;
Once drinking deep of that divinest anguish,
How could I seek the empty world again?

Though A. G. A. was by nature incapable of repentance, or
even of sustained remorse, haunting memories visited her with
increasing frequency as she grew older, which neither ambition,
multitudinous love affairs, nor her strong will to happiness could
wholly still. The beloved bluebell on the hillside was a sharp re-
minder of her lost child.

Sacred watcher, wave thy bells![4]
Fair hill flower and woodland child!
Dear to me in deep green dells—
Dearest on the mountains wild.

Bluebell, even as all divine
I have seen my darling shine—
Bluebell, even as wan and frail
I have seen my darling fail—
Thou hast found a voice for me,
And soothing words are breathed by thee.

Thus they murmur, "Summer's sun
Warms me till my life is done.
Would I rather choose to die
Under winter's ruthless sky?

"Glad I bloom and calm I fade;
Weeping twilight dews my bed;
Mourner, mourner, dry thy tears—
Sorrow comes with lengthened years!"

[4] The manuscript of this poem, initialed "E." and dated May 9, 1839,
is headed "A. G. A.   To the Bluebell." A canceled manuscript showing
variations in text is headed "To a Bluebell by A. G. A."

An old guitar called up the memory of a hapless youth who died of love for her, but the pity is for herself rather than for him.

> For him who struck thy foreign string,[5]
> I ween this heart hath ceased to care;
> Then why dost thou such feelings bring
> To my sad spirit, old guitar?
>
> It is as if the warm sunlight
> In some deep glen should lingering stay,
> When clouds of tempest and of night
> Had wrapt the parent orb away.
>
> It is as if the glassy brook
> Should image still its willows fair,
> Though years ago the woodman's stroke
> Laid low in dust their gleaming hair.
>
> Even so, guitar, thy magic tone
> Has moved the tear and waked the sigh,
> Has bid the ancient torrent flow
> Although its very source is dry!

A long-lost ring recovered from overgrowing grass was to her a "mute remembrancer" of crime.

> What winter floods, what showers of spring[6]
> Have drenched the grass by night and day;
> And yet, beneath, that spectre ring,
> Unmoved and undiscovered lay
> A mute remembrancer of crime,
> Long lost, concealed, forgot for years,
> It comes at last to cancel time,
> And waken unavailing tears.

[5] The manuscript, initialed "E." and dated August 30, 1838, is headed "A. G. A." Through another poem, dated January 6, 1840, and headed "F. De Samara. Written in the Gaaldine Prison Caves to A. G. A." ("Thy sun is near meridian height"), the guitar is identified with Fernando De Samara.

[6] The manuscript of this poem, dated March 27, 1839, is headed "A. G. A."

The sight and voice of a stranger spoke to her of one associated with the happier "years gone by."

> Where were ye all? and where wert thou?[7]
> I saw an eye that shone like thine;
> But dark curls waved around his brow,
> And his stern glance was strange to mine.
>
> And yet a dreamlike comfort came
> Into my heart and anxious eye;
> And, trembling yet to hear his name,
> I bent to listen watchfully.
>
> His voice, though never heard before,
> Still spoke to me of years gone by;
> It seemed a vision to restore
> That brought the hot tears to my eye.

Her own harp, which once gave her solace and joy, now repeated only "long-forgotten things" that darkened all her summer skies.

> Harp of wild and dream-like strain,[8]
> When I touch thy strings,
> Why dost thou repeat again
> Long-forgotten things?
>
> Harp, in other, earlier days,
> I could sing to thee;
> And not one of all my lays
> Vexed my memory.
>
> But now, if I awake a note
> That gave me joy before,
> Sounds of sorrow from thee float,
> Changing evermore.

---

[7] The poem, dated October, 1838, bears the heading "A. G. A." It is the first of a group of three on the manuscript page. (See chap. II, note 5.)

[8] The manuscript has disappeared from sight. The text is taken from Clement Shorter's transcript as printed in 1910.

Yet, still steeped in memory's dyes,
They come sailing on,
Darkening all my summer skies,
Shutting out my sun.

Youthful dreams were now but a memory yielding nought but care.

O Dream, where art thou now?[9]
Long years have past away
Since last, from off thine angel brow
I saw the light decay.

Alas, alas for me
Thou wert so bright and fair,
I could not think thy memory
Would yield me nought but care!

The sun-beam and the storm,
The summer-eve divine,
The silent night of solemn calm,
The full moon's cloudless shine,

Were once entwined with thee,
But now with weary pain,
Lost vision! 'tis enough for me—
Thou canst not shine again.

Worst of all were the thousand memories which came to haunt her in the dead of night.

I'll come when thou are saddest,[10]
Laid alone in the darkened room;
When the mad day's mirth has vanished,
And the smile of joy is banished
From evening's chilly gloom.

[9] The manuscript of this poem, dated November 5, 1838, carries no heading.

[10] The poem, undated and without heading, follows, on the manuscript sheet, "The night is darkening round me," which is dated November, 1837. On the reverse of the sheet are canceled versions of three poems, among them the canceled variant of "Song by Julius Angora."

I'll come when the heart's real feeling
Has entire, unbiassed sway,
And my influence o'er thee stealing,
Grief deepening, joy congealing,
Shall bear thy soul away.

Listen, 'tis just the hour,
The awful time for thee;
Dost thou not feel upon thy soul
A flood of strange sensations roll,
Forerunners of a sterner power,
Heralds of me?

Even sleep brought no relief from haunting memories.

Sleep brings no joy to me,[11]
Remembrance never dies;
My soul is given to misery
And lives in sighs.

Sleep brings no rest to me;
The shadows of the dead
My waking eyes may never see
Surround my bed.

Sleep brings no hope to me;
In soundest sleep they come,
And with their doleful imagery
Deepen the gloom.

Sleep brings no strength to me,
No power renewed to brave,
I only sail a wilder sea,
A darker wave.

Sleep brings no friend to me
To soothe and aid to bear;

[11] This poem, dated November, 1837, carries the heading "A. G. A." and is the second of three on a sheet, the reverse of which carries the poems dated October, 1838 (see note 7, above).

They all gaze, oh, how scornfully,
And I despair.

Sleep brings no wish to knit
My harassed heart beneath;
My only wish is to forget
In sleep of death.

CHAPTER XI

Fernando De Samara

THE GUITAR which disturbed Augusta's memory once belonged to Fernando De Samara, a youth of Areon Hall in Gaaldine, who on sailing for Gondal bade farewell to his foster sister[1] and sweetheart in the strongest possible avowals of fidelity.

> Now trust a heart that trusts in you,[2]
> And firmly say the word "Adieu";
> Be sure, wherever I may roam,
> My heart is with your heart at home;
>
> Unless there be no truth on earth,
> And vows meant true are nothing worth,
> And mortal man have no control
> Over his own unhappy soul;
>
> Unless I change in every thought,
> And memory will restore me nought,
> And all I have of virtue die
> Beneath far Gondal's Foreign sky.

[1] This detail develops from following poems.

[2] This poem, dated November, 1837, precedes on the manuscript sheet "Sleep brings no joy to me" (see chap. X, note 11). It carries no heading, but its close connection with the other Fernando poems fixes its place in this series.

The mountain peasant loves the heath
Better than richest plains beneath;
He would not give one moorland wild
For all the fields that ever smiled;

And whiter brows than yours may be,
And rosier cheeks my eyes may see,
And lightning looks from orbs divine
About my pathway burn and shine;

But that pure light, changeless and strong,
Cherished and watched and nursed so long;
That love that first its glory gave
Shall be my pole star to the grave.

In Gondal, under Augusta's charm, all the eventualities which
Fernando had thought of as impossibilities came to pass. Dazzled
by the light of her "orbs divine," he forgot his home, his foster
mother, and his sweetheart. All he had of virtue died, and for her
smile he cast away "virtue and faith and heaven." The story is
continued pathetically by the girl he betrayed and concluded
dramatically by Fernando himself.

O mother, I am not regretting[3]
To leave this wretched world below,
If there be nothing but forgetting
In that dark land to which I go.

Yet though 'tis wretched now to languish,
Deceived and tired and hopeless here,
No heart can quite repress the anguish
Of leaving things that once were dear.

Twice twelve short years, and all is over,
10 And day and night to rise no more;
And never more to be a rover
Along the fields, the woods, the shore;

[3] The manuscript of this poem, dated December 14, 1837, carries no
heading, but is fully identified by the place name "Areon's forest" and the
personal name "Fernando" in the text. The first 12 verses are written on
one side of the sheet and the remainder on the reverse, followed by "Why
do I hate that lone green dell?"

And never more at early dawning
To watch the stars of midnight wane;
To breathe the breath of summer morning
And see its sunshine ne'er again.

I hear the Abbey bells are ringing:
Methinks their chime-sound faint and drear,
Or else the wind is adverse winging,
20 And wafts its music from my ear.

The wind the winter night is speaking
Of thoughts and things that should not stay;
Mother, come near; my heart is breaking;
I cannot bear to go away.

And I *must* go whence no returning
To soothe your grief or calm your care;
Nay, do not weep: that bitter mourning
Tortures my soul with wild despair.

No; tell me that, when I am lying
30 In the old church beneath the stone,
You'll dry your tears and check your sighing,
And soon forget the spirit gone.

You've asked me long to tell what sorrow
Has blanched my cheek and quenched my eye;
And we shall sever ere to-morrow,
So I'll confess before I die.

Ten years ago in last September
Fernando left his home and you,
And still I think you must remember
40 The anguish of that last adieu;

And well you know how, wildly pining,
I longed to see his face again
Through all the Autumn's drear declining,
Its stormy nights and days of rain.

Down on the skirts of Areon's forest
There lies a lone and lovely glade;
And there the hearts together nourished
Their first, their fatal parting made.

The afternoon, in softened glory,
50 Bathed each green swell and waving tree;
Beyond the broad park, spread before me,
Stretched far away the boundless sea.

And there I stood, when he had left me,
With ashy cheek but tearless eye,
Watching the ship whose sail bereft me
Of life and hope and peace and joy.

It past; that night I sought a pillow
Of sleepless woe, and grieving lone
My soul still hovered o'er the billow,
60 And mourned a love for ever flown.

Yet, smiling bright in recollection,
One blissful hour returns to me:
One letter told of firm affection,
Of safe deliverance from the sea;

But not another. Fearing, hoping,
Spring, winter, harvest, glided o'er;
And time at length brought power for coping
With thoughts I could not once endure.

And I would seek in summer's evening
70 The place that saw our last farewell;
And there, a chain of visions weaving,
I'd linger till the curfew bell.

The picture of his betrayed sweetheart is repeated by Fernando
in a plaint to A. G. A., whom he addresses as Alcona.

Alcona, in its changing mood[4]
My soul will sometimes overfly
The long, long years of solitude
That 'twixt our time of meeting lie.

[4] The manuscript of this poem, dated September 6, 1839, carries no head-
ing, but the place name "Areon Hall" and the text identify it as the first
of Fernando's plaints to his seductress, whom he addresses as Alcona, which
is the territorial designation for Rosina. Since the heading of "Thy sun is
near meridian height" ("F. De Samara . . . to A. G. A.") makes it certain
that his seductress is A. G. A., it follows that Rosina and A. G. A. are one.
(See Introduction, p. 27.)

Hope and despair in turns arise
This doubting, dreading heart to move;
And now, 'mid smiles and bitter sighs,
Tell how I fear, tell how I love.

And now I say, "In Areon Hall—"
10 (Alas that such a dream should come,
When well I know, whate'er befall,
That Areon is no more my home.)

Yet, let me say, "In Areon Hall
The first faint red of morning shines,
And one right gladly to its call
The restless breath of grief resigns.

Her faded eye, her pallid face,
Would woo the soft, awaking wind;
All earth is breathing of the peace
20 She long has sought but cannot find.

How sweet it is to watch the mist
From that bright silent lake ascend,
And high o'er wood and mountain crest
With heaven's grey clouds as greyly blend.

How sweet it is to mark those clouds
Break brightly in the rising day;
To see the sober veil that shrouds
This summer morning melt away.

O sweet to some, but not to her;
30 Unm [ark] edst once at Nature's shrine,
She now kneels down a worshipper,
A mad adorer, love, to thine.

The time is come when hope, that long
Revived and sank, at length is o'er;
When faith in him, however strong,
Dare prompt her to believe no more.

The tears which day by day o'erflowed
Their heart-deep source begin to freeze;
And, as she gazes on the road
40 That glances through those spreading trees,

No throbbing flutter checks her breath
To mark a horseman hastening by;
Her haggard brow is calm as death,
And cold like death her dreary eye."

However sad the fate of the girl Fernando betrayed, his own
was infinitely more tragic, for A. G. A., when her brief interest
had run its course, banished him to "the Gaaldine prison caves,"
where he had long months to repent his folly and sin, and to call
down retribution upon his seductress.

Thy sun is near meridian height,[5]
And my sun sinks in endless night;
But, if that night bring only sleep,
Then I shall rest, while thou wilt weep.

And say not that my early tomb
Will give me to a darker doom:
Shall these long, agonising years
Be punished by eternal tears?

No; *that* I feel can never be;
10   A God of *hate* could hardly bear
To watch through all eternity
His own creations dread despair!

The pangs that wring my mortal breast,
Must claim from Justice lasting rest;
Enough, that this departing breath
Will pass in anguish worse than death.

If I have sinned, long, long ago
That sin was purified by woe:
I've suffered on through night and day;
20   I've trod a dark and frightful way.

Earth's wilderness was round me spread;
Heaven's tempests beat my naked head;

---

[5] The manuscript of this poem, initialed "E." and dated January 6, 1840,
has the heading "F. De Samara.   Written in the Gaaldine Prison Caves to
A.G.A."

I did not kneel: in vain would prayer
Have sought one gleam of mercy there!

How could I ask for pitying love,
When that grim concave frowned above,
Hoarding its lightnings to destroy
My only and my priceless joy?

They struck—and long may Eden shine
30 Ere I would call its glories mine:
All Heaven's undreamt felicity
Could never blot the past from me.

No; years may cloud and death may sever,
But what is done is done for ever;
And thou, false friend and treacherous guide,[6]
Go, sate thy cruel heart with pride.

Go, load my memory with shame;
Speak but to curse my hated name;
My tortured limbs in dungeons bind,
40 And spare my life to kill my mind.

Leave me in chains and darkness now;
And when my very soul is worn,
When reason's light has left my brow,
And madness cannot feel thy scorn,

Then come again—thou wilt not shrink;
I know thy soul is free from fear—
The last full cup of triumph drink,
Before the blank of death be there.

Thy raving, dying victim see,
50 Lost, cursed, degraded, all for thee!
Gaze on the wretch, recall to mind
His golden days left long behind.

Does memory sleep in Lethean rest?
Or wakes its whisper in thy breast?
O memory, wake! Let scenes return
That even her haughty heart must mourn!

[6] Compare Angelica's accusations of A. G. A. in "The Death of A. G. A.,"
lines 79–81 and 91–92.

Reveal, where o'er a lone green wood
The moon of summer pours,
Far down from heaven, its silver flood,
60 On deep Elderno's shores.

There, lingering in the wild embrace
Youth's warm affections gave,
She sits and fondly seems to trace
His features in the wave.

And while on that reflected face
Her eyes intently dwell,
"Fernando, sing to-night," she says,
"The lays I love so well."

He smiles and sings, though every air
70 Betrays the faith of yesterday;
His soul is glad to cast for her
Virtue and faith and Heaven away.

Well thou hast paid me back my love!
But if there be a God above
Whose arm is strong, whose word is true,
This hell shall wring thy spirit too!

At last Fernando, like Lord Alfred, took his own life in vain
effort to free himself from his enslaving love for A. G. A., dying
with her picture in his hand and in his heart.

Light up thy halls! 'Tis closing day;[7]
I'm drear and lone and far away—
Cold blows on my breast the northwind's bitter sigh,
And oh, my couch is bleak beneath the rainy sky!

Light up thy halls—and think not of me;
That face is absent now, thou hast hated so to see—
Bright be thine eyes, undimmed their dazzling shine,
For never, never more shall they encounter mine!

The desert moor is dark; there is tempest in the air;
10 I have breathed my only wish in one last, one burning prayer—

[7] The manuscript of this poem, dated November 1, 1838, and initialed
"E.," is headed "F. De Samara to A. G. A."

A prayer that would come forth, although it lingered long;
That set on fire my heart, but froze upon my tongue.

And now, it shall be done before the morning rise:
I will not watch the sun ascend in yonder skies.
One task alone remains—thy pictured face to view;
And then I go to prove if God, at least, be true!

Do I not see thee now? Thy black resplendent hair;
Thy glory-beaming brow, and smile, how heavenly fair!
Thine eyes are turned away—those eyes I would not see;
20 Their dark, their deadly ray, would more than madden me.

There, go, Deceiver, go! My hand is streaming wet;
My heart's blood flows to buy the blessing—To forget!
Oh could that lost heart give back, back again to thine,
One tenth part of the pain that clouds my dark decline!

Oh could I see thy lids weighed down in cheerless woe;
Too full to hide their tears, too stern to overflow;
Oh could I know thy soul with equal grief was torn,
This fate might be endured—this anguish might be borne!

How gloomy grows the night! 'Tis Gondal's wind that blows;
30 I shall not tread again the deep glens where it rose—
I feel it on my face—"Where, wild blast, dost thou roam?
What do we, wanderer, here, so far away from home?

"I do not need thy breath to cool my death-cold brow;
But go to that far land, where she is shining now;
Tell Her my latest wish, tell Her my dreary doom;
Say that *my* pangs are past, but *Hers* are yet to come."

Vain words—vain, frenzied thoughts! No ear can hear
      me call—
Lost in the vacant air my frantic curses fall—
And could she see me now, perchance her lip would smile,
40 Would smile in careless pride and utter scorn the while!

And yet for all her hate, each parting glance would tell
A stronger passion breathed, burned, in this last farewell.
Unconquered in my soul the Tyrant rules me still;
Life bows to my control, but *Love* I cannot kill!

Long afterward the picture which dropped from Fernando's dying hands was picked up by one who knew its history.

> Long neglect has worn away[8]
> Half the sweet enchanting smile;
> Time has turned the bloom to grey;
> Mould and damp the face defile.
>
> But that lock of silky hair,
> Still beneath the picture twined,
> Tells what once those features were,
> Paints their image on the mind.
>
> Fair the hand that traced that line,
> "Dearest, ever deem me true";
> Swiftly flew the fingers fine
> When the pen that motto drew.

[8] This poem, one of several on a sheet, has neither date nor heading, but the reverse of the sheet carries the date August, 1837. (See chap. III, note 2.)

CHAPTER XII

The Death of a Queen

WEARY OF PALACE and court, Augusta one day slipped out for a few hours of solitude on Elmor moors, attended only by Lord Lesley and Fair Surry, lovers absorbed in each other. Asleep in the sunshine, she was discovered by her onetime stepdaughter and old enemy, Angelica, wandering in the same wild region. Unprotected as the queen was, Angelica would have killed her with a knife had Augusta not just then awakened with such a dreary sigh that Angelica preferred to let her live on in her misery. An hour later, repenting the decision, Angelica sought the help of Douglas, a fellow outlaw, "to send to hell my mortal foe," promising him her love in return. Fair Surry and Lord Lesley died first, that in their deaths Augusta might "drain a deeper cup of bitterer pain." Then the queen went down under Douglas's knife, fighting savagely.

Angelica, her revenge accomplished, treacherously disappeared, leaving Douglas alone with his victim.

The queen's body, white and still in the moonlight, was found by Lord Eldred, Captain of the Queen's Guard. Watching beside it while his men pursued Douglas, Lord Eldred reviewed in memory the stormy life of his beloved ward and queen.

> Were they shepherds, who sat all day[1]
> On that brown mountain-side?
> But neither staff nor dog had they,
> Nor woolly flock to guide.

[1] The manuscript of this poem, initialed "E. J.," is headed "The Death of

They were clothed in savage attire;
Their locks were dark and long;
And at each belt a weapon dire,
Like bandit-knife, was hung.

One was a woman, tall and fair;
10 A princess she might be,
From her stately form, and her features rare,
And her look of majesty.

But, oh, she had a sullen frown,
A lip of cruel scorn,
As sweet tears never melted down
Her cheeks since she was born!

'Twas well she had no sceptre to wield,
No subject land to sway:
Fear might have made her vassals yield,
20 But Love had been far away.

Yet, Love was even at her feet
In his most burning mood:
That Love which will the Wicked greet
As kindly as the Good—

And he was noble too, who bowed
So humbly by her side,
Entreating, till his eyes o'erflowed,
Her spirit's icy pride.

"Angelica, from my very birth
30 I have been nursed in strife:
And lived upon this weary Earth
A wanderer, all my life.

"The baited tiger could not be
So much athirst for gore:

A. G. A." and carries dates of its beginning and completion, January, 1841, and May, 1844, showing that it was more than three years in the writing. The longest of Emily's poems, a narrative containing numerous reminiscent passages, it is the beginning point and reference guide in reconstructing the life story and character of the brilliant but puzzling heroine of this group of the Gondal poems.

For men and laws have tortured me
Till I can bear no more.

"The guiltless blood upon my hands
Will shut me out from Heaven;
And here, and even in foreign lands,
40 I cannot find a haven.

"And in all space, and in all time,
And through Eternity,
To aid a Spirit lost in crime,
I have no hope but thee.

"Yet will I swear, No saint on high
A truer faith could prove;
No angel, from that holy sky,
Could give thee purer love.

"For thee, through never-ending years,
50 I'd suffer endless pain;
But—only give me back my tears;
Return my love again!"

Many a time, unheeded, thus
The reckless man would pray;
But something woke an answering flush
On his lady's brow to-day;
And her eye flashed flame, as she turned to speak,
In concord with her reddening cheek:

"I've known a hundred kinds of love:
60 *All* made the loved one rue;
And what is thine that it should prove,
Than other love, more true?

"Listen; I've known a burning heart
To which my own was given;
Nay, not in passion; do not start—
Our love was love from heaven;
At least, if heavenly love be born
In the pure light of childhood's morn—
Long ere the poison-tainted air
70 From this world's plague-fen rises there.

"That heart was like a tropic sun
That kindles all it shines upon;
And never Magian devotee
Gave worship half so warm as I;
And never radiant bow could be
So welcome in a stormy sky.
My soul dwelt with her day and night:
She was my all-sufficing light,
My childhood's mate, my girlhood's guide,
80 My only blessing, only pride.

"But cursed be the very earth
That gave that fiend her fatal birth!
With her own hand she bent the bow
That laid my best affections low,
Then mocked my grief and scorned my prayers
And drowned my bloom of youth in tears.
Warnings, reproaches, both were vain—
What recked she of another's pain?
My dearer self she would not spare—
90 From Honour's voice she turned his ear:
First made her love his only stay,
Then snatched the treacherous prop away.
Douglas, he pleaded bitterly;
He pleaded as *you* plead to me
For lifelong chains or timeless tomb
Or any but an Exile's doom.
We both were scorned—both sternly driven
To shelter 'neath a foreign heaven;
And darkens o'er that dreary time
100 A wildering dream of frenzied crime.
I will not now those days recall;
The oath within that caverned hall
And its fulfilment, those you know—
We both together struck the blow.
But—you can never know the pain
That my lost heart did then sustain,
When severed wide by guiltless gore
I felt that *one* could love no more!
Back, maddening thought!—The grave is deep

146]

110 Where my Amedeus lies asleep,
And I have long forgot to weep.

"Now hear me: in these regions wild
I saw to-day my enemy.
Unarmed, as helpless as a child
She slumbered on a sunny lea.
Two friends—no other guard had she,
And they were wandering on the braes
And chasing in regardless glee
The wild goat o'er his dangerous ways.
120 My hand was raised—my knife was bare;
With stealthy tread I stole along;
But a wild bird sprang from his hidden lair
And woke her with a sudden song.
Yet moved she not: she only raised
Her lids and on the bright sun gazed,
And uttered such a dreary sigh
I thought just then she should not die
Since living was such misery.
Now, Douglas, for our hunted band—
130 For future joy and former woe—
Assist me with thy heart and hand
To send to hell my mortal foe.
Her friends fall[2] first, that she may drain
A deeper cup of bitterer pain.
Yonder they stand and watch the waves
Dash in among the echoing caves—
Their farewell sight of earth and sea!
Come, Douglas, rise and go with me."

.   .   .   .[3]

The lark sang clearly overhead,
140 And sweetly hummed the bee;
And softly, round their dying bed,
The wind blew from the sea.

[2] Hatfield has *fell*, but the manuscript is plainly *fall*.
[3] The line of dots and other such lines later in the poem apparently do not indicate ellipses; they are possibly Emily's device for showing passage of time and change of mood.

Fair Surry would have raised her eyes
To see that water shine;
To see once more in mountain skies
The summer sun decline:

But ever, on her fading cheek,
The languid lid would close,
As weary that such light should break
150 Its much-desired repose.

And she was waning fast away—
Even Memory's voice grew dim;
Her former life's eventful day
Had dwindled to a dream;

And hardly could her mind recall
One thought of joy or pain;
That cloud was gathering over all
Which never clears again.

In vain, in vain; you need not gaze
160 Upon those features now!
That sinking head you need not raise,
Nor kiss that pulseless brow.

Let out the grief that chokes your breath;
Lord Lesley, set it free:
The sternest eye, for such a death,
Might fill with sympathy.

The tresses o'er her bosom spread
Were by a faint breeze blown:
"Her heart is beating," Lesley said;
170 "She is not really gone!"

And still that form he fondly pressed;
And still of hope he dreamed;
Nor marked how from his own young breast
Life's crimson current streamed.

At last, the sunshine left the ground;
The laden bee flew home;
The deep down sea, with sadder sound,
Impelled its waves to foam;

And the corpse grew heavy on his arm,
180 The starry heaven grew dim,
The summer night, so mild and warm,
Felt wintery chill to him.

A troubled shadow o'er his eye
Came down, and rested there;
The moors and sky went swimming by,
Confused and strange and drear.

He faintly prayed, "Oh, Death, delay
Thy last fell dart to throw,
Till I can hear my Sovereign say,
190 'The traitors' heads are low!'

"God, guard her life, since not to me
That dearest boon was given;
God, bless her arm with victory
Or bless not me with heaven!"

Then came the cry of agony,
The pang of parting pain;
And he had overpassed the sea
That none can pass again.

.   .   .   .

Douglas leaned above the well,
200 Heather banks around him rose;
Bright and warm the sunshine fell
On that spot of sweet repose,

With the blue heaven bending o'er,
And the soft wind singing by,
And the clear stream evermore
Mingling harmony.

On the shady side reclined,
He watched its waters play,
And sound and sight had well combined
210 To banish gloom away.

A voice spoke near: "She'll come," it said,
"And, Douglas, thou shalt be
My love, although the very dead
Should rise to rival thee!

"Now, only let thine arm be true
And nerved, like mine, to kill;
And Gondal's royal race shall rue
This day on Elmor Hill!"

They wait not long; the rustling heath
220 Betrays their royal foe;
With hurried step and panting breath
And cheek almost as white as death,
Augusta sprang below—

Yet marked she not where Douglas lay;
She only saw the well—
The tiny fountain, churning spray
Within its mossy cell.

"Oh, I have wrongs to pay," she cried,
"Give life, give vigour now!"
230 And, stooping by the water's side,
She drank its crystal flow.

And brightly, with that draught, came back
The glory of her matchless eye,
As, glancing o'er the moorland track,
She shook her head impatiently.

Nor shape, nor shade—the mountain flocks
Quietly feed in grassy dells;
Nor sound, except the distant rocks
Echoing to their bells.

240 She turns—she meets the Murderer's gaze;
Her own is scorched with a sudden blaze—
The blood streams down her brow;
The blood streams through her coal-black hair—
She strikes it off with little care;
She scarcely feels it flow;
For she has marked and known him too
And his own heart's ensanguined dew
Must slake her vengeance now!

False friend! no tongue save thine can tell
250 The mortal strife that then befell;

But, ere night darkened down,
The stream in silence sang once more;
And, on its green bank, bathed in gore,
Augusta lay alone!

False Love! no earthly eye did see,
Yet Heaven's pure eye regarded thee,
Where thy own Douglas bled—
How thou didst turn in mockery
From his last hopeless agony,
260 And leave the hungry hawk to be
Sole watcher of the dead!

  .   .   .   .

Was it a deadly swoon?
Or was her spirit really gone?
And the cold corpse, beneath the moon,
Laid like another mass of dust and stone?

The moon was full that night,
The sky was almost like the day:
You might have seen the pulse's play
Upon her forehead white;

270 You might have seen the dear, dear sign of life
In her uncovered eye,
And her cheek changing in the mortal strife
Betwixt the pain to live and agony to die.

But nothing mutable was there;
The face, all deadly fair,
Showed a fixed impress of keen suffering past,
And the raised lid did show
No wandering gleam below
But a stark anguish, self-destroyed at last.

280 Long he gazed and held his breath,
Kneeling on the blood-stained heath;
Long he gazed those lids beneath
Looking into Death!

Not a word from his followers fell:
They stood by, mute and pale;

That black treason uttered well
Its own heart-harrowing tale.

But earth was bathed in other gore:
There were crimson drops across the moor;
290 And Lord Eldred, glancing round,
Saw those tokens on the ground:

"Bring him back!" he hoarsely said;
"Wounded is the traitor fled;
Vengeance may hold but minutes brief,
And you have all your lives for grief."

He is left alone—he sees the stars
Their quiet course continuing,
And, far away, down Elmor scars
He hears the stream its waters fling.

300 That lulling monotone did sing
Of broken rock and shaggy glen,
Of welcome for the moorcock's wing;
But, not of wail for men!

Nothing in heaven or earth to show
One sign of sympathizing woe—
And nothing but that agony,
In her now unconscious eye,
To weigh upon the labouring breast
And prove she did not pass at rest.

310 But he who watched, in thought had gone,
Retracing back her lifetime flown:
Like sudden ghosts, to memory came
Full many a face and many a name,
Full many a heart, that, in the tomb,
He almost deemed might have throbbed again,
Had they but known her dreary doom,
Had they but seen their idol there,
A wreck of desolate despair,
Left to the wild birds of the air
320 And mountain winds and rain.
For him— no tear his stern eye shed
As he looked down upon the dead.

"Wild morn," he thought, "and doubtful noon;
    But yet it was a glorious sun,
    Though comet-like its course was run.
    That sun should never have been given
    To burn and dazzle in the heaven,
    Or night has quenched it far too soon!

"And thou art gone—with all thy pride;
330 Thou, so adored, so deified!
    Cold as the earth, unweeting now
    Of love, or joy, or mortal woe.
    For what thou wert I would not grieve,
    But much for what thou wert to be—
    That life so stormy and so brief,
    That death has wronged us more than thee.
    Thy passionate youth was nearly past,
    The opening sea seemed smooth at last;
    Yet vainly flowed the calmer wave
340 Since fate had not decreed to save.
    And vain too must the sorrow be
    Of those who live to mourn for thee;
    But Gondal's foes shall not complain
    That thy dear blood was poured in vain!"

Douglas, though wounded, outdistanced his pursuers, until high on a crag he found himself trapped at last, facing a chasm bridged only by a giant pine "laid by the mountain men." By dislodging this tree and sending it crashing downward, he started an avalanche which buried his enemies.

Well, narrower draw the circle round,[4]
    And hush that organ's solemn sound;
    And quench the lamp, and stir the fire
    To rouse its flickering radiance higher;
    Loop up the window's velvet veil
    That we may hear the night-wind wail;
    For wild those gusts, and well their chimes
    Blend with a song of troubled times—

[4] The manuscript of this poem, dated July 11, 1838, is headed "Douglas's Ride."

What rider up Gobelrin's glen
10 Has spurred his straining steed,
And fast and far from living men
Has pressed with maddening speed?

I saw his hoof-prints mark the rock
When swift he left the plain;
I heard deep down the echoing shock
Re-echo back again.

From cliff to cliff, through rock and heath,
That coal-black courser bounds;
Nor heeds the river pent beneath,
20 Nor marks how fierce it sounds.

With streaming hair and forehead bare
And mantle waving wide,
His master rides; the eagles there
Soar up on every side;

The goats fly by with timid cry,
Their realm so rashly won,
They pause—he still ascends on high;
They gaze—but he is gone.

O gallant horse, hold on thy course!
30 The road is tracked behind—
Spur, rider, spur, or vain thy force;
Death comes on every wind.

Roared thunder loud from that pitchy cloud?
From it the torrents flow;
Or, woke the breeze in the swaying trees
That frown so dark below?

He breathes at last, when the valley is past;
He rests on the grey rock's brow—
What ails thee, steed? At thy master's need,
40 Wilt thou prove faithless now?

No; hardly checked, with ears erect,
The charger champed his rein,

Ere his quivering limbs, all foam-beflecked,
Were off like light again.

Hark; through the pass, with threatening crash,
Comes on the increasing roar!
But what shall brave the deep, deep wave—
The deadly path before?

Their feet are dyed in a darker tide
50 Who dare those dangers drear;
Their breasts have burst through the battle's worst,
And why should they tremble here?

Strong hearts they bear, and arms as good,
To conquer or to fall;
They dash into the boiling flood,
They gain the rock's steep wall—

"Now, my bold men, this one pass more,
This narrow chasm of stone,
And Douglas, for our sovereign's gore,
60 Shall yield us back his own."

I hear their ever-nearing tread
Sound through the granite glen;
There is a tall pine overhead
Laid by the mountain men.

That dizzy bridge, which no horse could track,
Has choked the outlaw's way;
There, like a wild beast, he turns back,
And grimly stands at bay.

Why smiles he so, when far below
70 He sees the toiling chase?
The ponderous tree sways heavily
And totters from its place.

They raise their eyes, for the sunny skies
Are lost in sudden shade;
But, Douglas neither shrinks nor flies—
He need not fly the dead.

The story of Douglas's escape took on the accents of dark
legend.

> O hinder me by no delay,[5]
> My horse is weary of the way;
> And still his breast must stem the tide
> Whose waves are foaming far and wide.
> Leagues off I heard their thundering roar,
> As fast they burst upon the shore:
> A stronger steed than mine might dread
> To brave them in their boiling bed.
>
> Thus spoke the traveller, but in vain:
> The stranger would not turn away;
> Still clung she to his bridle rein,
> And still entreated him to stay.

> And now the house-dog stretched once more[6]
> His limbs upon the glowing floor;
> The children half resumed their play,
> Though from the warm hearth scared away.
> The goodwife left her spinning-wheel,
> And spread with smiles the evening meal;
> The shepherd placed a seat and pressed
> To their poor fare his unknown guest.
> And he unclasped his mantle now,
> 10 And raised the covering from his brow;
> Said, "Voyagers by land and sea
> Were seldom feasted daintily";
> And checked his host by adding stern
> He'd no refinement to unlearn.
> A silence settled on the room;
> The cheerful welcome sank to gloom;
> But not those words, though cold and high,

[5] The poem, without date or heading, follows on the same manuscript
sheet "The wide cathedral aisles are lone," which bears the date March,
1838 (see chap. VI, note 8); though not identified, it and the following
poem are possibly part of the story of Douglas's escape.

[6] This manuscript, dated July 12, 1839, and signed "E. J. Brontë," bears
no identifying heading.

So froze their hospitable joy.
No—there was something in his face,
20 Some nameless thing they could not trace,
And something in his voice's tone
Which turned their blood as chill as stone.
The ringlets of his long black hair
Fell o'er a cheek most ghastly fair.
Youthful he seemed—but worn as they
Who spend too soon their youthful day.
When his glance drooped, 'twas hard to quell
Unbidden feelings' sudden swell;
And pity scarce her tears could hide,
30 So sweet that brow, with all its pride;
But when upraised his eye would dart
An icy shudder through the heart.
Compassion changed to horror then
And fear to meet that gaze again.
It was not hatred's tiger-glare,[7]
Nor the wild anguish of despair;
It was not useless misery
Which mocks at friendship's sympathy.
No—lightning all unearthly shone
40 Deep in that dark eye's circling zone,
Such withering lightning as we deem
None but a spectre's look may beam;
And glad they were when he turned away
And wrapt him in his mantle grey,
Leant down his head upon his arm
And veiled from view their [sic] basilisk charm.

For all her vivid personality, for all her charm and her evil deeds, for all the love and hate lavished upon her, Augusta was soon forgotten by both friends and enemies. Only Lord Eldred

[7] It sometimes happens that Emily in two poems concerning the same person, though written years apart, will use a similar, or the same, descriptive phrase or word. Compare Douglas's statement of himself in "The Death of A. G. A.":

> The baited tiger could not be
> So much athirst for gore,

with the present phrase, "hatred's tiger-glare."

carried her image in his heart and grieved for her through the years.

How few, of all the hearts that loved,[8]
Are grieving for thee now!
And why should mine, to-night, be moved
With such a sense of woe?

Too often, thus, when left alone
Where none my thoughts can see,
Comes back a word, a passing tone
From thy strange history.

Sometimes I seem to see thee rise,
10 A glorious child again—
All virtues beaming from thine eyes
That ever honoured men—

Courage and Truth, a generous breast
Where Love and Gladness lay;
A being whose very Memory blest
And made the mourner gay.

O, fairly spread thy early sail,
And fresh and pure and free
Was the first impulse of the gale
20 That urged life's wave for thee!

Why did the pilot, too confiding,
Dream o'er that Ocean's foam,
And trust in Pleasure's careless guiding
To bring his vessel home?

For well he knew what dangers frowned,
What mists would gather dim;
What rocks and shelves and sands lay round
Between his port and him.

[8] The manuscript of this poem, dated March 11, 1844, and initialed "E.," carries the heading "E. W. to A. G. A." The E. W. is evidently Lord Eldred W. Compare the first and last stanzas with "Written in Aspin Castle" ("How do I love on summer nights"), lines 84–91, and "The Death of A. G. A.," lines 310–320.

The very brightness of the sun,
30 The splendour of the main,
The wind that bore him wildly on
Should not have warned in vain.

An anxious gazer from the shore,
I marked the whitening wave,
And wept above thy fate the more
Because I could not save.

It recks not now, when all is over;
But yet my heart will be
A mourner still, though friend and lover
40 Have both forgotten thee!

The linnet in the rocky dells,[9]
The moor-lark in the air,
The bee among the heather-bells
That hide my lady fair:

The wild deer browse above her breast;
The wild birds raise their brood;
And they, her smiles of love caressed,
Have left her solitude!

I ween, that when the grave's dark wall
Did first her form retain,
They thought their hearts could ne'er recall
The light of joy again.

They thought the tide of grief would flow
Unchecked through future years,
But where is all their anguish now,
And where are all their tears?

Well, let them fight for Honour's breath,
Or Pleasure's shade pursue—
The Dweller in the land of Death
Is changed and careless too.

[9] The manuscript, dated May 1, 1844, has no heading, but is signed "E. W." [Lord Eldred W.].

And if their eyes should watch and weep
Till sorrow's source were dry,
She would not, in her tranquil sleep,
Return a single sigh.

Blow, west wind, by the lonely mound,
And murmur, summer streams,
There is no need of other sound
To soothe my Lady's dreams.

Appendixes

APPENDIX I

Emily Brontë's Poems Pertaining to the Republican-Royalist War in Gondal

Emily and Anne Brontë's poems and birthday notes, read together, make it clear that, though their writing through the summer of 1845 was still concerned with the A. G. A.–Julius period, the play itself, with a new generation of Gondalans on the stage, was absorbed in a bitter civil war between Royalists and Republicans.

As early as July 30, 1841, Emily wrote, "The Gondalians are at present in a threatening state, but there is no open rupture as yet," and on October 2, 1844, she translates this general condition into the plaint ("D. G. C. to J. A.") of a young man facing the coming crisis. There is no futher reference to the rift until Emily's poem of June 2, 1845—and that a doubtful one. But the struggle looms large in the birthday notes of July of that year. Emily records that during a three-day excursion to York— "our first long journey by ourselves together"—she and Anne dramatized themselves as a group of young Royalists escaping from the palaces of instruction to join their families and friends, "hard driven at present by the victorious Republicans." In evident gusto she adds, "The Gondals still flourish bright as ever. . . . We intend sticking firm by the rascals as long as they delight us, which I am glad to say they do at present."

Anne on the same day, after remarking that Emily is "writing the Emperor Julius's life," continues in a contrasting tone of weariness and depression, "The Republicans are uppermost, but the Royalists are not quite overcome. The young sovereigns, with their brothers and sisters, are still at the Palace of Instruction. . . . The Gondals in general are not in first-rate playing condition. Will they improve?"

After the note celebrating her twenty-seventh birthday, Emily wrote but four poems, three of them certainly of the Royalist-Republican war, the other very probably so. Although the last is but a first draft, it shows touches of the supreme greatness reached in the closing A. G. A.–Julius poems.

E.   D. G. C. to J. A.[1]   October 2, 1844

Come, the wind may never again
Blow as now it blows for us;
And the stars may never again shine as now they shine;
Long before October returns,
Seas of blood will have parted us;
And you must crush the love in your heart, and I the love in mine!

For face to face will our kindred stand,
And as they are so shall we be;
Forgetting how the same sweet earth has borne and nourished all—
One must fight for the people's power,
And one for the rights of Royalty;
And each be ready to give his life to work the other's fall.

[1] The manuscript of this poem is the earliest, both in plot sequence and in date of composition, to be identified with the Republican-Royalist conflict. Nothing more is known either of the speaker or the friend he addresses.

On September 12, 1846, Anne Brontë completed a companion poem of 150 lines signed "E. Z." ("I dreamt last night, and in that dream"), which has as climax the stanza:

> Back, foolish tears! the man I slew
>   Was not the boy I cherished so;
> And that young arm that clasped the friend
>   Was not the same that stabbed the foe;
> By time and adverse thoughts estranged,
> And wrongs and vengeance, both were changed.

The chance of war we cannot shun,
Nor would we shrink from our fathers' cause,
Nor dread Death more because the hand that gives it may be dear;
We must bear to see Ambition rule
Over Love, with his iron laws;
Must yield our blood for a stranger's sake, and refuse ourselves a tear!

So, the wind may never again
Blow as now it blows for us,
And the stars may never again shine as now they shine;
Next October, the cannon's roar
From hostile ranks may be urging us—
Me to strike for your life's blood, and you to strike for mine.

June 2, 1845

How beautiful the Earth is still[2]
To thee—how full of Happiness;
How little fraught with real ill
Or shadowy phantoms of distress;

How Spring can bring thee glory yet
And Summer win thee to forget
December's sullen time!
Why dost thou hold the treasure fast
Of youth's delight, when youth is past
10 And thou art near thy prime?

When those who were thy own compeers,
Equal in fortunes and in years,
Have seen their morning melt in tears,
To dull unlovely day;
Blest, had they died unproved and young
Before their hearts were wildly wrung,
Poor slaves, subdued by passions strong,
A weak and helpless prey!

[2] The manuscript of this poem has no identifying heading. At the end is written in Charlotte's hand, "Never was better stuff penned." In tone and spirit the poem is so like "No coward soul is mine" that I take it to be another expression of the credo of that speaker, a Gondalan facing a crisis incident to the Republican-Royalist conflict.

"Because, I hoped while they enjoyed,
20 And by fulfilment, hope destroyed—
As children hope, with trustful breast,
I waited Bliss and cherished Rest.

"A thoughtful Spirit taught me soon
That we must long till life be done;
That every phase of earthly joy
Will always fade and always cloy—

"This I foresaw, and would not chase
The fleeting treacheries,
But with firm foot and tranquil face
30 Held backward from the tempting race,
Gazed o'er the sands the waves efface
To the enduring seas—

"There cast my anchor of Desire
Deep in unknown Eternity;
Nor ever let my Spirit tire
With looking for *What is to be.*

"It is Hope's spell that glorifies
Like youth to my maturer eyes
All Nature's million mysteries—
40 The fearful and the fair—

"Hope soothes me in the griefs I know,
She lulls my pain for others' woe
And makes me strong to undergo
What I am born to bear.

"Glad comforter, will I not brave
Unawed the darkness of the grave?
Nay, smile to hear Death's billows rave,
My Guide, sustained by thee?
The more unjust seems present fate
50 The more my Spirit springs elate
Strong in thy strength, to anticipate
Rewarding Destiny!"

August, 1845

M. A.   WRITTEN ON THE DUNGEON WALL—N. C.[3]

I know that tonight the wind is sighing,
The soft August wind, over forest and moor;
While I in a grave-like chill am lying
On the damp black flags of my dungeon-floor.

I know that the Harvest Moon is shining:
She neither will wax nor wane for me;
Yet I weary, weary with vain repining,
One gleam of her heaven-bright face to see!

For this constant darkness is wasting the gladness,
10 Fast wasting the gladness of life away:
It gathers up thoughts akin to madness
That never would cloud the world of day.

I chide with my soul—I bid it cherish
The feelings it lived on when I was free,
But shrinking it murmurs, "Let Memory perish,
Forget, for thy friends have forgotten thee!"

Alas, I did think that they were weeping
Such tears as I weep—it is not so!
Their careless young eyes are closed in sleeping;
20 Their brows are unshadowed, undimmed by woe.

Might I go to their beds, I'd rouse that slumber;
My spirit should startle their rest, and tell
How, hour after hour, I wakefully number
Deep buried from light in my lonely cell!

Yet, let them dream on, though dreary dreaming
Would haunt my pillow if *they* were here,
And *I* were laid warmly under the gleaming
Of that guardian moon and her comrade star.

---

[3] Apparently the speaker in this poem is a young Royalist, prisoner in the Northern College. Anne repeats the situation and theme in a group of addresses and answers between a Royalist lover, "A. E.," and his sweetheart, "Zerona L." ("Weep not too much, my darling").

Better that I, my own fate mourning,
30 Should pine alone in the prison-gloom,
Than waken free on the summer morning
And feel they were suffering this awful doom.

M. A.

October 9, 1845

JULIAN M. AND A. G. ROCHELLE[4]

Silent is the House—all are laid asleep;
One, alone, looks out o'er the snow wreaths deep;
Watching every cloud, dreading every breeze
That whirls the 'wildering drifts and bends the groaning
trees.

[4] The theme of this poem, a young girl in prison, was foreshadowed some years earlier in the undated and unidentified fragment, canceled by Emily:

> Iernë's eyes were glazed and dim
> When the castle bell tolled one.
> She looked around her dungeon grim;
> The grating cast a doubtful gleam;
> 'Twas one cloud-saddened cold moon-beam.
> Iernë gazed as in a dream
> And thought she saw the sun.
>
> She thought it was the break of day,
> The night had been so long.

From the present 152 lines, Emily lifted 13–44 and 65–92, for inclusion in *Poems*, 1846. Charlotte, in preparing a small group of her sister's poems for publishing with *Wuthering Heights* in 1850, combined lines 1–12 with eight of her own composition to make "The Visionary." It was not until 1938 that the full poem saw print, in a small volume transcribed by Helen Brown and Joan Mott from Emily's notebook headed "Gondal Poems." Three years later, in Hatfield's edition of 1941, it made its first appearance in an inclusive volume of Emily's poems.

Its cryptic third stanza has an interesting parallel in Anne's poem of a few days earlier—Zerona L.'s farewell to her lover, A. E., as prison closes around him ("Oh, weep not, love! each tear that springs"):

> A mother's sad, reproachful eye,
> A father's scowling brow—
> But he may frown and she may sigh:
> I will not break my vow.

Cheerful is the hearth, soft the matted floor;
Not one shivering gust creeps through pane or door;
The little lamp burns straight, its rays shoot strong and far;
I trim it well to be the Wanderer's guiding-star.

Frown, my haughty sire; chide, my angry dame;
10 Set your slaves to spy, threaten me with shame:
But neither sire nor dame, nor prying serf shall know
What angel nightly tracks that waste of winter snow.

In the dungeon crypts idly did I stray,
Reckless of the lives wasting there away;
"Draw the ponderous bars; open, Warder stern!"
He dare not say me nay—the hinges harshly turn.

"Our guests are darkly lodged," I whispered, gazing through
The vault whose grated eye showed heaven more grey than
blue.
(This was when glad spring laughed in awaking pride.)
20 "Aye, darkly lodged enough!" returned my sullen guide.

Then, God forgive my youth, forgive my careless tongue!
I scoffed, as the chill chains on the damp flagstones rung;
"Confined in triple walls, art thou so much to fear,
That we must bind thee down and clench thy fetters here?"

The captive raised her face; it was as soft and mild
As sculptured marble saint or slumbering, unweaned child;
It was so soft and mild, it was so sweet and fair,
Pain could not trace a line nor grief a shadow there!

The captive raised her hand and pressed it to her brow:
30 "I have been struck," she said, "and I am suffering now;
Yet these are little worth, your bolts and irons strong;
And were they forged in steel they could not hold me long."

Hoarse laughed the jailor grim: "Shall I be won to hear;
Dost think, fond dreaming wretch, that *I* shall grant thy
prayer?
Or, better still, wilt melt my master's heart with groans?
Ah, sooner might the sun thaw down these granite stones!

"My master's voice is low, his aspect bland and kind,
But hard as hardest flint the soul that lurks behind;

And I am rough and rude, yet not more rough to see
40 Than is the hidden ghost which has its home in me!"

About her lips there played a smile of almost scorn:
"My friend," she gently said, "you have not heard me mourn;
When you my parents' lives—*my* lost life, can restore,
Then may I weep and sue—but *never*, Friend, before!"

Her head sank on her hands; its fair curls swept the ground;
The dungeon seemed to swim in strange confusion round—
"Is she so near to death?" I murmured, half aloud,
And, kneeling, parted back the floating golden cloud.

Alas, how former days upon my heart were borne;
50 How memory mirrored then the prisoner's joyous morn:
Too blithe, too loving child, too warmly, wildly gay!
Was that the wintry close of thy celestial May?

She knew me and she sighed, "Lord Julian, can it be,
Of all my playmates, you alone remember me?
Nay, start not at my words, unless you deem it shame
To own, from conquered foe, a once familiar name.

"I cannot wonder now at ought the world will do,
And insult and contempt I lightly brook from you,
Since those, who vowed away their souls to win my love,
60 Around this living grave like utter strangers move!

"Nor has one voice been raised to plead that I might die,
Not buried under earth but in the open sky;
By ball or speedy knife or headsman's skilful blow—
A quick and welcome pang instead of lingering woe!

"Yet, tell them, Julian, all, I am not doomed to wear
Year after year in gloom and desolate despair;
A messenger of Hope comes every night to me,
And offers, for short life, eternal liberty.

"He comes with western winds, with evening's wandering
            airs,
70 With that clear dusk of heaven that brings the thickest stars;
Winds take a pensive tone, and stars a tender fire,
And visions rise and change which kill me with desire—

"Desire for nothing known in my maturer years
   When joy grew mad with awe at counting future tears;
   When, if my spirit's sky was full of flashes warm,
   I knew not whence they came, from sun or thunderstorm;

"But first a hush of peace, a soundless calm descends;
   The struggle of distress and fierce impatience ends;
   Mute music soothes my breast—unuttered harmony
80 That I could never dream till earth was lost to me.

"Then dawns the Invisible, the Unseen its truth reveals;
   My outward sense is gone, my inward essence feels—
   Its wings are almost free, its home, its harbour found;
   Measuring the gulf it stoops and dares the final bound!

"Oh, dreadful is the check—intense the agony
   When the ear begins to hear and the eye begins to see;
   When the pulse begins to throb, the brain to think again,
   The soul to feel the flesh and the flesh to feel the chain!

"Yet I would lose no sting, would wish no torture less;
90 The more that anguish racks the earlier it will bless;
   And robed in fires of Hell, or bright with heavenly shine,
   If it but herald Death, the vision is divine."

She ceased to speak, and I, unanswering, watched her there,
   Not daring now to touch one lock of silken hair—
   As I had knelt in scorn, on the dank floor I knelt still,
   My fingers in the links of that iron hard and chill.

I heard, and yet heard not, the surly keeper growl;
   I saw, yet did not see, the flagstone damp and foul.
   The keeper, to and fro, paced by the bolted door
100 And shivered as he walked and, as he shivered, swore.

While my cheek glowed in flame, I marked that he did rave
   Of air that froze his blood, and moisture like the grave—
   "We have been two hours good!" he muttered peevishly;
   Then, loosing off his belt the rusty dungeon key,

He said, "You may be pleased, Lord Julian, still to stay,
   But duty will not let me linger here all day;
   If I might go, I'd leave this badge of mine with you,
   Not doubting that you'd prove a jailor stern and true."

I took the proffered charge; the captive's drooping lid
110 Beneath its shady lash a sudden lightning hid:
Earth's hope was not so dead, heaven's home was not so
    dear;
I read it in that flash of longing quelled by fear.

Then like a tender child whose hand did just enfold,
Safe in its eager grasp, a bird it wept to hold,
When pierced with one wild glance from the troubled hazel
    eye,
It gushes into tears and lets its treasure fly,

Thus ruth and selfish love together striving tore
The heart all newly taught to pity and adore;
If I should break the chain, I felt my bird would go;
120 Yet I must break the chain or seal the prisoner's woe.

Short strife, what rest could soothe—what peace could visit
    me
While she lay pining there for Death to set her free?
"Rochelle, the dungeons teem with foes to gorge our hate—
Thou art too young to die by such a bitter fate!"

With hurried blow on blow, I struck the fetters through,
Regardless how that deed my after hours might rue.
Oh, I was over-blest by the warm unasked embrace—
By the smile of grateful joy that lit her angel face!

And I was over-blest—aye, more than I could dream
130 When, faint, she turned aside from noon's unwonted beam;
When though the cage was wide—the heaven around
    it lay—
Its pinion would not waft my wounded dove away.

Through thirteen anxious weeks of terror-blent delight
I guarded her by day and guarded her by night,
While foes were prowling near and Death gazed greedily
And only Hope remained a faithful friend to me.

Then oft with taunting smile I heard my kindred tell
"How Julian loved his hearth and sheltering roof-tree well;
How the trumpet's voice might call, the battle-standard
    wave,
140 But Julian had no heart to fill a patriot's grave."

And I, who am so quick to answer sneer with sneer;
So ready to condemn, to scorn, a coward's fear,
I held my peace like one whose conscience keeps him dumb,
And saw my kinsmen go—and lingered still at home.

Another hand than mine my rightful banner held
And gathered my renown on Freedom's crimson field;
Yet I had no desire the glorious prize to gain—
It needed braver nerve to face the world's disdain.

And by the patient strength that could that world defy,
150 By suffering, with calm mind, contempt and calumny;
By never-doubting love, unswerving constancy,
Rochelle, I earned at last an equal love from thee!

January 2, 1846

No coward soul is mine[5]
No trembler in the world's storm-troubled sphere
I see Heaven's glories shine
And Faith shines equal arming me from Fear

O God within my breast
Almighty ever-present Deity
Life, that in me hast rest
As I Undying Life, have power in Thee

Vain are the thousand creeds
That move men's hearts, unutterably vain,
Worthless as withered weeds
Or idlest froth amid the boundless main

To waken doubt in one
Holding so fast by thy infinity
So surely anchored on
The steadfast rock of Immortality

[5] This manuscript is the last entry in Emily's untitled notebook. Written immediately following the completion of her contribution to *Poems* by Currer, Ellis, and Acton Bell, it marks, apparently, her return to the civil war epic, interrupted by Charlotte's discovery of "Gondal Poems" in the preceding October. Though usually read as a subjective poem, spoken by Emily in the first person, evidence indicates that it was spoken by a Gondalan facing a crisis incident to the Republican-Royalist conflict.

With wide-embracing love
Thy spirit animates eternal years
Pervades and broods above,
Changes, sustains, dissolves, creates and rears

Though Earth and moon were gone
And suns and universes ceased to be
And thou wert left alone
Every Existence would exist in thee

There is not room for Death,
Nor atom that his might could render void
Since thou art Being and Breath
And what thou art may never be destroyed.

14 September, 1846

Why ask to know the date—the clime?[6]
More than mere words they cannot be:
Men knelt to God and worshipped crime,
And crushed the helpless, even as we.

[6] This untitled manuscript, entered in "Gondal Poems" on September 14, 1846, is Emily's last verse. (But see note 8, following.) *Poems* a failure in the eyes of the public, and *Wuthering Heights* still hunting a publisher, she turned again to "tortured Gondal," now raised to the universal, any country caught in fraternal strife—

When kindred strive—God help the weak!
A brother's ruth 'tis vain to seek.

While all other poems in Emily's two notebooks of 1844 are fair copies, this is an unfinished first draft, indescribably scratched and interlined, with one turn of plot balanced against another. Punctuation, largely disregarded, has been supplied here, to assist the reading.

Earlier, on the third and fourth of September, 1845, Anne wrote two companion poems, illustrating the sentence in her note of July 31 of that year, "The Gondals are at present in a sad state. The Republicans are uppermost, but the Royalists are not quite overcome."

SONG

We know where deepest lies the snow,
And where the frost-winds keenest blow
    On every mountain brow.
We long have known and learnt to bear
The wandering outlaw's toil and care,

But they had learnt, from length of strife
Of civil war and anarchy,
To laugh at death and look on life
With somewhat lighter sympathy.

It was the autumn of the year,
10 The time to labouring peasants dear;
Week after week, from noon to noon,
September shone as bright as June—
Still, never hand a sickle held;
The crops were garnered in the field—
Trod out and ground by horses' feet
While every ear was milky sweet;
And kneaded on the threshing-floor
With mire of tears and human gore.
Some said they thought that heaven's pure rain
20 Would hardly bless those fields again:
Not so—the all-benignant skies
Rebuked that fear of famished eyes—

But where we late were hunted, there
    Our foes are hunted now.

We have their princely homes, and they
To our wild haunts are chased away,
    Dark woods, and desert caves;
And we can range from hill to hill,
And chase our vanquished victors still,
Small respite will they find, until
    They slumber in their graves.

But I would rather be the hare
That, crouching in its sheltered lair,
    Must start at every sound;
That, forced from cornfields waving wide,
Is driven to seek the bare hillside,
Or in the tangled copse-wood hide,
    Than be the hunter's hound!
                        September 3, 1845.

SONG

Come to the banquet; triumph in your songs!
    Strike up the chords, and sing of "Victory!"
The oppressed have risen to redress their wrongs,
    The Tyrants are o'erthrown, the Land is free!
The Land is free! Aye, shout it forth once more;
Is she not red with her oppressors' gore?

July passed on with showers and dew,
And August glowed in showerless blue;
No harvest time could be more fair
Had harvest fruits but ripened there.

And I confess that hate of rest,
And thirst for things abandoned now,
Had weaned me from my country's breast
30 And brought me to that land of woe.

Enthusiast—in a name delighting,
My alien sword I drew to free
One race, beneath two standards, fighting
For Loyalty and Liberty—

We are her champions; shall we not rejoice?
    Are not the tyrants' broad domains our own?
Then wherefore triumph with a faltering voice?
    And talk of freedom in a doubtful tone?
Have we not longed through life the reign to see
Of Justice, linked with Glorious Liberty?

Shout you that will, and you that can rejoice
    To revel in the riches of your foes.
In praise of deadly vengeance lift your voice;
    Gloat o'er your tyrants' blood, your victims' woes.
I'd rather listen to the skylark's songs,
And think on Gondal's and my father's wrongs.

It may be pleasant to recall the death
    Of those beneath whose sheltering roof you lie;
But I would rather press the mountain-heath
    With nought to shield me from the starry sky.
And dream of yet untasted Victory;
A distant hope; and feel that I am free!

Oh, happy life! To rove the mountains wild,
    The waving woods, or ocean's heaving breast,
With limbs unfettered, conscience undefiled,
    And choosing where to wander, where to rest!
Hunted, opposed, but ever strong to cope
With toils and perils; ever full of hope!

"Our flower is budding." When that word was heard
    On desert shore, or breezy mountain's brow;
Wherever said, what glorious thoughts it stirred!
    'Twas budding then; say, "Has it blossomed now?"
Is *this* the end we struggled to obtain?
Oh, for the wandering Outlaw's life again!
                                    A. B., September 4, 1845.

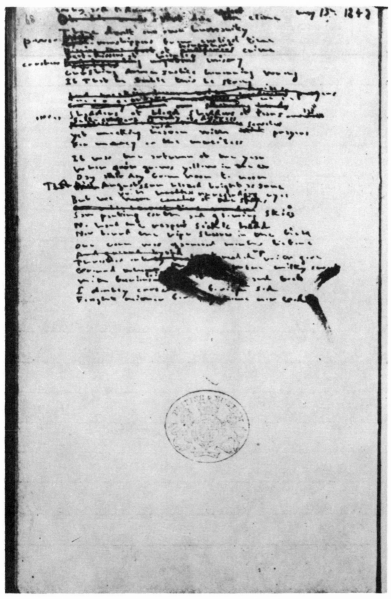

Last extant lines by Emily Brontë, concluding her notebook headed "Gondal Poems"

Emily's journal fragment written on Branwell's twentieth birthday, the drawing showing herself and Anne at work on the Gondal creation

When kindred strive—God help the weak!
A brother's ruth 'tis vain to seek:
At first, it hurt my chivalry
To join them in their cruelty;
But I grew hard—I learnt to wear
40 An iron front to terror's prayer;
I learnt to turn my ears away
From torture's groans, as well as they.
By force I learnt—What power had I
To say the conquered should not die?
What heart, one trembling foe to save
When hundreds daily filled the grave?
Yet, there *were* faces that could move
A moment's flash of human love;
And there were fates that made me feel
50 I was not, to the centre, steel—
I've often witnessed wise men fear
To meet distress which they foresaw; .
And seeming cowards nobly bear
A doom that thrilled the brave with awe.

Strange proofs I've seen, how hearts could hide
Their secret with a life-long pride,
And then reveal it as they died—
Strange courage, and strange weakness too,
In that last hour when most are true,
60 And timid natures strangely nerved
To deeds from which the desperate swerved.
These I may tell; but, leave them now:
Go with me where my thoughts would go;
Now all to-day and all last night
I've had one scene before my sight—

Wood-shadowed dales, a harvest moon
Unclouded in its glorious noon;
A solemn landscape wide and still;
A red fire on a distant hill—
70 A line of fires, and deep below
Another dusker, drearier glow—
Charred beams, and lime, and blackened stones
Self-piled in cairns o'er burning bones,

And lurid flames that licked the wood,
Then quenched their glare in pools of blood.

But yester-eve—No! never care;
Let street and suburb smoulder there—
Smoke-hidden in the winding glen
They lay too far to vex my ken.

80 Four score shot down—all veterans strong;
One prisoner spared—their leader—young,
And he within his house was laid
Wounded and weak and nearly dead.
We gave him life against his will,
For he entreated us to kill—
But statue-like we saw his tears—
And harshly fell our captain's sneers!

"Now, heaven forbid!" with scorn he said,
"That noble gore our hands should shed
90 Like common blood—retain thy breath,
Or scheme if thou canst purchase death.
When men are poor we sometimes hear
And pitying grant that dastard prayer;
When men are rich we make them buy
The pleasant privilege to die.
O, we have castles reared for kings,
Embattled towers and buttressed wings
Thrice three feet thick and guarded well
With chain and bolt and sentinel!
100 We build our despots' dwellings sure
Knowing they love to live secure—
And our respect for royalty
Extends to thy estate and thee!"

The suppliant groaned; his moistened eye
Swam wild and dim with agony.
The gentle blood could ill sustain
Degrading taunts, unhonoured pain.

Bold had he shown himself to lead;
Eager to smite and proud to bleed;
110 A man amid the battle's storm:
An infant in the after calm.

Beyond the town his mansion stood
Girt round with pasture-land and wood;
And there our wounded soldiers lying
Enjoyed the ease of wealth in dying.

For him, no mortal more than he
Had softened life with luxury;
And truly did our priest declare
"Of good things he had had his share."

120 We lodged him in an empty place,
The full moon beaming on his face
Through shivered glass and ruins, made
Where shell and ball the fiercest played.

I watched his ghastly couch beside
Regardless if he lived or died—
Nay, muttering curses on the breast
Whose ceaseless moans denied me rest.

'Twas hard, I know, 'twas harsh to say
"Hell snatch thy worthless soul away!"
130 But then 'twas hard my lids to keep
Through the long night estranged from sleep.
Captive and keeper both outworn
Each in his misery yearned for morn,
Even though returning morn should bring
Intenser toil and suffering.

Slow, slow it came! Our dreary room
Grew drearier with departing gloom;
Yet as the west wind warmly blew
I felt my pulses bound anew,
140 And turned to him—Nor breeze, nor ray
Revived that mould of shattered clay.
Scarce conscious of his pain he lay—
Scarce conscious that my hands removed
The glittering toys his lightness loved—
The jewelled rings and locket fair
Where rival curls of silken hair
Sable and brown revealed to me
A tale of doubtful constancy.

"Forsake the world without regret,"
150 I murmured in contemptuous tone;
  "The world, poor wretch, will soon forget
  Thy noble name when thou art gone!
  Happy, if years of slothful shame
  Could perish like a noble name—
  If God did no account require
  And being with breathing might expire!"
  And words of such contempt I said,
  Harsh insults o'er a dying bed,
  Which as they darken memory now
160 Disturb my pulse and flush my brow.
  I know that Justice holds in store
  Reprisals for those days of gore;
  Not for the blood but for the sin
  Of stifling mercy's voice within.

  The blood spilt gives no pang at all;
  It is my conscience haunting me,
  Telling how oft my lips shed gall
  On many a thing too weak to be,
  Even in thought, my enemy;
170 And whispering ever, when I pray,
  "God will repay—God will repay!"

  He does repay and soon and well
  The deeds that turn his earth to hell,
  The wrongs that aim a venomed dart
  Through nature at the Eternal Heart.
  Surely my cruel tongue was cursed.
  I know my prisoner heard me speak:
  A transient gleam of feeling burst
  And wandered o'er his haggard cheek,
180 And from his quivering lids there stole
  A look to melt a demon's soul—
  A silent prayer more powerful far
  Than any breathed petitions are,
  Pleading in mortal agony
  To mercy's Source but not to me.
  Now I recall that glance and groan
  And wring my hands in vain distress;

Then I was adamantine stone
Nor felt one touch of tenderness.

190 My plunder ta'en I left him there,
Without one breath of morning air
To struggle with his last despair,
Regardless of the 'wildered cry,
Which wailed for death, yea wailed to die.
I left him there unwatched, alone,
And eager sought the court below
Where o'er a trough of chiselled stone
An ice cold well did gurgling flow.
The water in its basin shed
200 A stranger tinge of fiery red.
I drank and scarcely marked the hue;
My food was dyed with crimson too.
As I went out, a ragged child
With wasted cheek and ringlets wild,
A shape of fear and misery,
Raised up her helpless hands to me
And begged her father's face to see.
I spurned the piteous wretch away
"Thy father's face is lifeless clay
210 As thine mayst be ere fall of day
Unless the truth be quickly told—
Where they have hid thy father's gold."
Yet in the intervals of pain
He heard my taunts and moaned again,
And mocking moans did I reply
And asked him why he would not die
In noble agony—uncomplaining.
Was it not foul disgrace and shame
To thus disgrace his ancient name?
220 Just then a comrade hurried in,
"Alas," he cried, "sin genders sin.
For every soldier slain they've sworn
To hang up five to-morrow morn.
They've ta'en of stranglers[7] sixty-three,
Full thirty from one company,

[7] Possibly written in mistake for "stragglers."

And all my father's family;
And comrade thou hadst only one—
They've ta'en thy all, thy little son."
Down at my captive's feet I fell—

230 I had no option in despair—
"As thou wouldst save thy soul from hell
My heart's own darling bid them spare,
Or human hate and hate divine
Blight every orphan flower of thine."
He raised his head—from death beguiled,
He wakened up—he almost smiled.
"I lost last night my only child.
Twice in my arms twice on my knee
You stabbed my child and laughed at me.
240 And so," with choking voice he said,
"I trust in God; I hope she's dead,
Yet not to thee, not even to thee
Would I return such misery.
Such is that fearful grief I know
I will not cause thee equal woe.
Write that they harm no infant there—
Write that it is my latest prayer."
I wrote—he signed—and thus did save
My treasure from the gory grave
250 And O my soul longed wildly then
To give his saviour life again.
But heedless of my gratitude
The silent corpse before me lay
And still methinks in gloomy mood
I see it fresh as yesterday,
The sad face raised imploringly
To mercy's God, and not to me.
I could not rescue him; his child
I found alive, and tended well
260 But she was full of anguish wild
And hated me like we hate hell
And weary with her savage woe
One moonless night I let her go.

In C. W. Hatfield's *Complete Poems of Emily Jane Brontë*
(1941), this note is appended to the above poem:

This poem was left in an incomplete state by the author. Lines 1 to 148 contain comparatively few alterations, and were probably copied from an earlier draft, but from line 149 onwards the alterations and cancellations are very numerous and much of the script is almost unreadable. Some of the printed words are partly conjectural.

Lines 149 to 156 and 172 to 189 are cancelled by lines drawn across them in the manuscript. A few almost illegible trial lines and parts of lines have been disregarded. . . .

Lines 1 to 8, 27 to 54, and 76 to 263 are now printed for the first time in an edition of the poems.

May 13, 1848

Why ask to know what date, what clime?[8]
There dwelt our own humanity,
Power-worshippers from earliest time,
Foot-kissers of triumphant crime
Crushers of helpless misery,
Crushing down Justice, honouring Wrong:
If that be feeble, this be strong.

Shedders of blood, shedders of tears:
Self-cursers avid of distress;
Yet mocking heaven with senseless prayers
For mercy on the merciless.

It was the autumn of the year
When grain grows yellow in the ear;
Day after day, from noon to noon,
The August sun blazed bright as June.

But we with unregarding eyes
Saw panting earth and glowing skies;

[8] The disturbing presence of Branwell in the parsonage, together with Emily's preoccupation with the publication of *Wuthering Heights*, probably accounts for the virtual closing of her poetry notebooks early in 1846. By May, 1848, it was evident that the public had rejected her novel; and on the thirteenth of that month she turned again to Gondal, in revision of the unfinished war narrative, carrying it through 25 lines, which are, indeed, so far as the records go, the last lines Emily Brontë wrote. (See illustration facing p. 176.)

Appendix I

No hand the reaper's sickle held,
Nor bound the ripe sheaves in the field.

Our corn was garnered months before,
Threshed out and kneaded-up with gore;
Ground when the ears were milky sweet
With furious toil of hoofs and feet;
I, doubly cursed on foreign sod,
Fought neither for my home nor God.

APPENDIX II

Emily and Anne Brontë's Prose Notes

1

This, the earliest of Emily and Anne Brontë's six prose notes, dates from Emily's seventeenth and Anne's fifteenth year. Its cryptic sentence, "The Gondal's are discovering the interior of Gaaldine," is the earliest extant mention of the Gondal play[1] and the fantastic world it created. Its critical importance overshadows even the graphic picture of routine parsonage life depicted in the rest of the note. It reveals that the original Gondal, "an island in the North Pacific," had been expanded by the discovery and exploration of Gaaldine, "a newly discovered island in the South Pacific," and it suggests that the younger girls were following a pattern set by Charlotte and Branwell's expansion of the original Glasstown Confederacy into the far-flung empire of Angria. It, regrettably, gives no evidence as to whether they had yet begun to reduce the play to literature.

The original manuscript of the note is in the Bonnell Collection, Brontë Museum, Haworth, England.

> November the 24 1834   Monday
> Emily Jane Brontë
> Anne Brontë

I fed Rainbow, Diamond Snowflake Jasper pheasent (alias)[2]   this morning Branwell went down to Mʳ Drivers and brought news that Sir

---

[1] Anne's list of Gondal place names in Goldsmith's *Grammar of Geography* is not dated.

[2] This second parenthesis is so dim as to be practically imaginary.

Robert Peel was going to be invited to stand for Leeds   Anne and I
have been peeling Apples for Charlotte to make an apple pudding and
for Aunts nuts and apples[3]   Charlotte said she made puddings per-
fectly and she was of a quick but lim[i]ted intellect   Taby said just
now Come Anne pilloputate (i e pill a potato [)]   Aunt has come into
the kitchen just now and said where are your feet Anne   Anne an-
swered On the floor Aunt   papa opened the parlour door and gave
Branwell a letter saying here Branwell read this and show it to your
Aunt and Charlotte—The Gondals are discovering the interior of
Gaaldine   Sally Mosley is washing in the back-kitchin

It is past Twelve o'clock   Anne and I have not tid[i]ed ourselves,
done our bed work or done our lessons and we want to go out to
play   we are going to have for Dinner Boiled Beef Turnips, potatoes
and applepudding. The kitchin is in a very untidy state   Anne and I
have not done our music exercise which consists of b major   Taby
said on my putting a pen in her face Ya pitter pottering there instead
of pilling a potate   I answered O Dear, O Dear, O Dear I will di-
rectly   with that I get up, take a knife and begin pilling (finished
pilling the potatoes [)]   papa going to walk   Mr Sunderland[4] ex-
pected

Anne and I say I wonder what we shall be like[5] and what we shall
be and where we shall be[6] if all goes on well in the year 1874—in
which year I shall be in my 54th year   Anne will be going in her 55th
year   Branwell will be going in his 58th year And Charlotte in her
59th year   hoping we shall all be well at that time we close our paper
Emily and Anne
November the 24 1834

2

It would seem that birthdays held peculiar significance for the
young Brontës, but as milestones in their lives or vantage points
directing their gaze into the future rather than as family festi-
vals. In the note that follows, Emily's crabbed, uneven hand-
printing records that her brother is entering upon his twentieth
year, but gives no hint of parsonage celebration—cake, candles,

---

[3] *Aunt's nuts and apples* now first deciphered.
[4] The last syllable of this name is uncertain.
[5] The original has *if all goes on well* canceled.
[6] *this year* canceled.

or presents. Perhaps it was enough for the young people that they were together and at home.

Branwell at this period was distinctly at loose ends, living at the parsonage, dependent upon his father. Charlotte, supporting herself as a teacher in Miss Wooler's school at Roe Head, and Anne, a pupil in the same school, were at home for the holidays. Emily either had not yet entered into the bondage of Miss Patchett's school at Halifax, or was at home on vacation.[7]

Here again it is the critical implications rather than biographical details that challenge interest. Less than a year earlier, on or before July 12, 1836, Emily wrote her first extant verse, launching a series which at the date of this note had grown to an even dozen pieces, seven definitely pertaining to the heroine of Gondal, Augusta Geraldine Almeda, carrying her story from birth through Elbë's death. Perhaps this is a clue to the contents of Volume I of "Agustus [*sic*] Almeda's life."

The original of this paper was acquired by the Brontë Society in 1951, and was first published in *Transactions* of that year. It is now in the Brontë Museum, Haworth, England.

Monday evening June 26 1837
at [a] bit past 4 o'clock   Charlotte working in Aunts room   Branwell reading Eugene Aram[8] to her   Anne and I writing in the drawing room—Anne a poem beginning "fair was the evening and brightly the sun["]19—I Agustus-Almedas[10] life 1st v. 1–4th page from the last a fine rather coolish thin grey cloudy but sunny day   Aunt working in the little Room   papa—gone out.   Tabby in the Kitchin—the Emperors and Empresses of Gondal and Gaaldine preparing to depart from Gaaldine to Gondal to prepare for the coronation[11] which will be on the 12th of July   Queen Vittiora [*sic*] ascended the throne this

[7] Charlotte's letter, reporting Emily's departure to Law Hill has been dated both April 2, 1837, and October 2, 1837.
[8] A three-volume novel by Edward George Earle Bulwer-Lytton, published in 1832.
[9] A narrative poem of 69 four-line stanzas, dated July 1, 1837, concerned with the separation and reunion of a youth and maiden, Alexander Hybernia and Alexandrina Zenobia.
[10] Agustus = Augusta?
[11] The coronation of Julius Brenzaida, Prince of Angora in Gondal and King of Almedore in Gaaldine, as joint sovereign with Gerald Exina, King of Gondal, in the great national cathedral. Eight months later, in March,

month[12]   Northangerland in Monceys Isle—Zamorna at Eversham.[13] all tight and right in which condition it is to be hoped we shall all be on this day 4 years at which time Charlotte will be 25 and 2 months— Branwell just 24 it being his birthday—myself 22 and 10 months and a peice [*sic*] Anne 21 and nearly a half   I wonder where we shall be and how we shall be and what kind of a day it will be then   let us hope for the best[14]

Emily Jane Brontë—Anne Brontë

Just below these lines is a pen-and-ink drawing of two female figures seated at a table, one labeled "Emily," the other "Anne." On the table is a box marked "the Tin Box" and two sheets marked "the papers" and "The papers." (See illustration facing p. 177.) Below and to the right of the drawing is the following continuation:

Aunt. Come Emily its past 4 o'clock   Emily, Yes Aunt   Anne Well do you intend to write in the evening   Emily well what think you (we agreed to go out 1st to make sure   if we get into a humor we may stay in [)]]
I guess that this day 4 years we shall all be in this drawing room com-

---

1838, Emily describes the scene in verse ("The wide cathedral aisles are lone"):

> Where Gondal's monarchs, bending low
> After the hush of silent prayer,
> Take, in heaven's sight, their awful vow,
> And never dying union swear.

In "His land may burst the galling chain," she continues the theme, picturing Gerald cast in depths of a dungeon by the false Julius, who, breaking his coronation oath, had made himself sole emperor of Gondal and Gaaldine.

[12] Alexandrina Victoria, only child of the Duke of Kent, succeeded her uncle, King William IV, to the throne of the United Kingdom of Great Britain and Ireland on June 20, 1837, and was crowned on June 28, 1838.

[13] *Northangerland . . . Eversham.* This sentence refers to current events of Charlotte and Branwell's Angrian play. Percy, Earl of Northangerland, had led a victorious rebellion against Arthur Wellesley, Duke of Zamorna and Emperor of Angria, taking him prisoner and banishing him to a distant island. Escaping *à la* Napoleon from Elba, Zamorna returned to Angria, rallied his subjects, and at "the Battle of Eversham," re-established himself firmly on his throne. Northangerland escaped to Moncey's Island, originally called Monkey's Island.

[14] Each of the extant notes or papers signed by Emily and Anne ends with a similar straining into the future—always hopeful.

fortable   I hope it may be so   Anne guesses we shall all be gone somewhere together comfortable   we hope it may be either [short word lost in the uneven edge of the paper].

3

On Emily's birthday, July 30, in both 1841 and 1845, she and Anne exchanged commonplace notes to be opened four years later, which are the chief prose sources of our knowledge of the Gondal play.

The originals of these notes being unavailable, Clement Shorter's transcripts, printed in *Charlotte Brontë and Her Circle*, 1896, are here used, corrected by several portions of the originals which he reproduced in facsimile.

A Paper to be opened

when Anne is

25 years old

or [on]my next birthday after—

if

—all be well—

Emily Jane Brontë   July the 30th 1841[15]

It is Friday evening—near 9 o'clock—wild rainy weather   I am seated in the dining room after having just concluded tidying our desk-boxes—writing this document   Papa is in the parlour. Aunt upstairs in her room. she has been[16] reading Blackwood's Magazine to papa. Victoria and Adelaide are ensconced in the peat-house. Keeper is in the kitchen. Hero in his cage. We are all stout and hearty as I hope is the case with Charlotte, Branwell, and Anne, of whom the first is at John White Esqre Upperwood House, Rawdon   The second is at Luddenden foot and the third's I believe at Scarborough—inditing perhaps, a paper corresponding to this.

A scheme is at present in agitation for setting us up in A School of our own   as yet nothing is determined but I hope and trust it may go on and prosper and answer our highest expectations. this day 4-years

---

[15] On either side of this heading is a pen-and-ink sketch of a female figure, presumably the author. To the left she is seated before a desk, writing; to the right she is looking out of a window, with the desk and vacated chair to her back and left.

[16] The original has *just been,* with *just* canceled.

Appendix II

I wonder whether we shall still be dragging on in our present condition or established to our hearts' content   Time will show—

I guess that at the time appointed for the opening of this paper—We (i e) Charlotte, Anne and I—shall[17] be all merrily[18] seated in our own sitting-room in some pleasant and flourishing seminary having just gathered in for the midsummer holidays   Our debts will be paid off and we shall have cash in hand to a considerable amount. papa Aunt and Branwell will either have been, or be coming—to visit us—it will be a fine warm [?][19] evening—very different from this bleak look-out [?][20] Anne and I will perchance slip out into the garden [?],[21] few minutes to piruse [sic] our papers. I hope either this or something better will be the case—

The Gondalians are at present in a threatening state but there is no open rupture as yet—all the princes and princesses of the royal [sic?] royaltys are at the Palace of Instruction. I have a good many books on hand, but I am sorry to say that—as usual I make small progress with any—however I have just made a new regularity paper! and I will[22] Verb Sap[23]—to do great things. and now I close sending from far an ex[hortation?][24] of courage [?][25] courage! to exiled and harrassed [sic] Anne & wishing she was here.

July the 30th, A.D. 1841

This is Emily's birthday. She has now completed her 23rd year, and is, I believe, at home. Charlotte is a governess in the family of Mr. White. Branwell is a clerk in the railroad station at Luddenden Foot, and I am a governess in the family of Mr. Robinson. I dislike the situation and wish to change it for another. I am now at Scarborough. My pupils are gone to bed and I am hastening to finish this before I follow them.

We are thinking of setting up a school of our own, but nothing definite is settled about it yet, and we do not know whether we shall be

---

[17] *will* canceled.
[18] This reading is doubtful.
[19] Word hidden under an ink spot.
[20] Word hidden under an ink spot.
[21] Word hidden under an ink spot.
[22] Reading doubtful.
[23] Probably Emily's abbreviation and application of the Latin phrase *Verbum sat sapienti est*—a word to the wise is sufficient.
[24] Word very dim.
[25] Indecipherable word canceled with heavy ink.

able to or not. I hope we shall. And I wonder what will be our condition and how or where we shall all be on this day four years hence; at which time, if all be well, I shall be 25 years and 6 months old, Emily will be 27 years old, Branwell 28 years and 1 month, and Charlotte 29 years and a quarter. We are now all separate and not likely to meet again for many a weary week, but we are none of us ill that I know of and all are doing something for our own livelihood except Emily, who, however, is as busy as any of us, and in reality earns her food and raiment as much as we do.

> How little know we what we are
> How less what we may be!

Four years ago I was at school. Since then I have been a governess at Blake Hall, left it, come to Thorp Green, and seen the sea and York Minster. Emily has been a teacher at Miss Patchet's school, and left it. Charlotte has left Miss Wooler's, been a governess at Mrs. Sidgwick's, left her, and gone to Mrs. White's. Branwell has given up painting, been a tutor in Cumberland, left it, and become a clerk on the railroad. Tabby has left us, Martha Brown has come in her place. We have got Keeper, got a sweet little cat and lost it, and also got a hawk. Got a wild goose which has flown away, and three tame ones, one of which has been killed. All these diversities, with many others, are things we did not expect or foresee in the July of 1837. What will the next four years bring forth? Providence only knows. But we ourselves have sustained very little alteration since that time. I have the same faults that I had then, only I have more wisdom and experience, and a little more self-possession than I then enjoyed. How will it be when we open this paper and the one Emily has written? I wonder whether the Gondaliand [*sic*] will still be flourishing, and what will be their condition. I am now engaged in writing the fourth volume of Solala Vernon's Life.

For some time I have looked upon 25 as a sort of era in my existence. It may prove a true presentiment, or it may be only a superstitious fancy; the latter seems most likely, but time will show.

Anne Brontë

4

Haworth, Thursday, July 30th, 1845

My birthday—showery, breezy, cool. I am twenty-seven years old to-day. This morning Anne and I opened the papers we wrote four years since, on my twenty-third birthday. This paper we intend, if all be well, to open on my thirtieth—three years hence, in 1848. Since the 1841 paper the following events have taken place. Our school scheme has been abandoned, and instead Charlotte and I went to Brussels on the 8th of February 1842.

Branwell left his place at Luddenden Foot. C. and I returned from Brussels, November 8th 1842, in consequence of aunt's death.

Branwell went to Thorp Green as a tutor, where Anne still continued, January 1843.

Charlotte returned to Brussels the same month, and, after staying a year, came back again on New Year's Day 1844.

Anne left her situation at Thorp Green of her own accord, June 1845.

Anne and I went [on] our first long journey by ourselves together, leaving home on the 30th of June, Monday, sleeping at York, returning to Keighley Tuesday evening, sleeping there and walking home on Wednesday morning. Though the weather was broken we enjoyed ourselves very much, except during a few hours at Bradford. And during our excursion we were, Ronald Macalgin, Henry Angora, Juliet Angusteena, Rosabella Esmalden, Ella and Julian Egremont, Catharine Navarre, and Cordelia Fitzaphnold, escaping from the palaces of instruction to join the Royalists who are hard driven at present by the victorious Republicans. The Gondals still flourish bright as ever   I am at present writing a work on the First Wars—Anne has been writing some articles on this and a book by Henry Sophona—We intend sticking firm by the rascals as long as they delight us which I am glad to say they do at present. I should have mentioned that last summer the School Scheme was revived in full vigour—We had prospectuses printed. despatched letters to all acquaintances imparting our plans and did our little all—but it was found no go—now I dont desire a school at all and none of us have any great longing for it. We have cash enough for our present wants with a prospect of accumulation— We are all in decent health. only that papa has a complaint in his eyes and with the exception of B who I hope will be better and do better, hereafter. I am quite contented for myself—not as idle as formerly, altogether as hearty and having learnt to make the most of the present and hope for the future with less fidgetness that I cannot do all I wish —seldom or ever troubled with nothing to [?][26] and merely desiring

---

[26] Indecipherable.

that every body could be as comfortable as myself and as undesponding and then we should have a very tolerable world of it.

By mistake I find we have opened the paper on the 31st instead of the 30th Yesterday was much such a day as this but the morning was divine—

Tabby who was gone in our last paper is come back and has lived with us—two years and a half and is in good health—Martha who also departed is here too—We have got Flossy, got and lost Tiger—lost the hawk Hero which with the geese was given away, and is doubtless dead, for when I came back from Brussels I inquired on all hands and could hear nothing of him. Tiger died early last year—Keeper and Flossy are well, also the canary acquired four years since. We are now all at home, and likely to be there some time. Branwell went to Liverpool on Tuesday to stay a week. Tabby has just been teasing me to turn as formerly to 'pilloputate.' Anne and I should have picked the black currants if it had been fine and sunshiny. I must hurry off now to my turning and ironing. I have plenty of work on hands, and writing, and am altogether full of business. With best wishes for the whole house till 1848, July 30th, and as much longer as may be,—I conclude. Emily Brontë.

Thursday, July the 31st, 1845.[27] Yesterday was Emily's birthday, and the time when we should have opened our 1845 paper, but by mistake we opened it to-day instead. How many things have happened since it was written—some pleasant, some far otherwise. Yet I was then at Thorp Green, and now I am only just escaped from it. I was wishing to leave it then, and if I had known that I had four years longer to stay how wretched I should have been; but during my stay I have had some very unpleasant and undreamt-of experiences of human nature. Others have seen more changes. Charlotte has left Mr. White's and been twice to Brussels, where she stayed each time nearly a year. Emily has been there too, and stayed nearly a year. Branwell has left Luddenden Foot, and been a tutor at Thorp Green, and had much tribulation and ill health. He was very ill on Thursday, but he went with John Brown to Liverpool, where he now is, I suppose; and we hope he will be better and do better in future. This is a dismal, cloudy, wet evening. We have had so far a very cold wet summer. Charlotte has lately been to Hathersage, in Derbyshire, on a visit of

[27] Anne's date differs from Emily's; Anne is correct—July 31, 1845, fell on a Thursday.

three weeks to Ellen Nussey. She is now sitting sewing in the dining-room. Emily is ironing upstairs. I am sitting in the dining-room in the rocking-chair before the fire with my feet on the fender. Papa is in the parlour. Tabby and Martha are, I think, in the kitchen. Keeper and Flossy are, I do not know where. Little Dick is hopping in his cage. When the last paper was written we were thinking of setting up a school. The scheme has been dropt, and long after taken up again and dropt again because we could not get pupils. Charlotte is thinking about getting another situation. She wishes to go to Paris. Will she go? She has let Flossy in, by-the-by, and he is now lying on the sofa. Emily is engaged in writing the Emperor Julius's life. She has read some of it, and I want very much to hear the rest. She is writing some poetry, too. I wonder what it is about? I have begun the third volume of Passages in the Life of an Individual. I wish I had finished it. This afternoon I began to set about making my grey figured silk frock that was dyed at Keighley. What sort of a hand shall I make of it? E. and I have a great deal of work to do. When shall we sensibly diminish it? I want to get a habit of early rising. Shall I succeed? We have not yet finished our Gondal Chronicles that we began three years and a half ago. When will they be done? The Gondals are at present in a sad state. The Republicans are uppermost, but the Royalists are not quite overcome. The young sovereigns, with their brothers and sisters, are still at the Palace of Instruction. The Unique Society, above half a year ago, were wrecked on a desert island as they were returning from Gaul.[28] They are still there, but we have not played at them much yet. The Gondals in general are not in first-rate playing condition. Will they improve? I wonder how we shall all be and where and how situated on the thirtieth of July 1848, when, if we are all alive, Emily will be just 30. I shall be in my 29th year, Charlotte in her 33rd, and Branwell in his 32nd; and what changes shall we have seen and known; and shall we be much changed ourselves? I hope not, for the worse at least. I for my part cannot well be flatter or older in mind than I am now. Hoping for the best, I conclude.

Anne Brontë

[28] Probably Shorter's rationalizing of Gaaldine.

5

A list of Gondal characters penciled in small hand-printing by Anne Brontë in two columns on the upper half of a scrap of paper measuring four by three inches.

Arthur Exina
Gerald Exina
Edward Hybernia
Gerald ——
Alexander ——
Halbert Clifford
Julia At [crossed out]
Archibald MacRay
Gerald F [crossed out]
Henry Sophona
Eustace Sophona
Adolphus St. Albert
Albert Vernon
Alexander D

Alexandria Zenobia Hybernia
Isabella Senland
Xirilla Senland
Lucia Angora
Catherina T G Angusteena
Isabella Abrantez
Eliza Hybernia
Harriet Eagle
Isidora Montara
Helen Douglas
Cornelia Alzerno
Rosalind Fizhorch

Indexes

Index of First Lines

Index of First Lines

Index of First Lines

General Index

A. G. A. *See* Almeda, Augusta Geraldine

Almeda, Augusta Geraldine: various appellations for, 20, 26–27, 43, 51, 52, 57, 59, 62, 82, 108, 120, 136; character of, 22–23, 41; birth and childhood, 47–51, 158; education of, 50–51; seduces and betrays Julius, 51–54; elopes with Elbë, 55; grieves for Elbë, 57–62, 65–67; imprisonment, 60–65; loves Lord Alfred S., 69–70; betrays Amedeus and Angelica, and dismisses Lord Alfred for Julius, 78–81, 82–92, 89–91, 101, 143–147; urges Julius to conquest, 93, 98; grieves for Julius, 111–112, 126–127; a fugitive, 120–124; exposes her child, 122–124; suffers remorse, 127–132; betrays Fernando De Samara, 133–142; death of, 143–160. *See also* Brenzaida, Julius

Angria: geography, 12–13; source of name, 13, evolution and history of, 13, 15, 21, 22, 24, 29, 38; magic in, 38. *See also* Glasstown; Gondal

Arabian Nights, 12

Ashley Library (British Museum), 18, 21

Berg Collection (New York Public Library), 19, 21

Bonnell, H. H., 16

Bonnell Collection (Brontë Museum, Haworth), 15, 16, 17–18

Branwell, Aunt Elizabeth, 16, 30, 186, 187, 188, 189

Brenzaida, Julius: various appellations for, 20, 43, 109; place in Gondal story, 41; imprisonment, 52–53; conquests of, 93–98, crowned Emperor, 98–99; betrays Gerald, 99–100; assassinated, 101–111; empire overthrown, 108–111. *See also* Almeda, Augusta Geraldine

Brontë, Anne: part in Gondal, 11, 15–16, 18–19, 22–23, 25, 28, 52, 55, 98, 164, 167, 168, 174–176, 185–195; journal fragments and birthday notes, 16, 22, 28, 29, 30, 185–195; literary remains, 17; lists Gondal place names, 18; Gondal poems (quoted or named), 19, 52, 55, 98, 164, 167, 168, 174–176; *Agnes Grey*, 30; part in "*Poems* by Currer, Ellis, and Acton Bell," 30–32; "Solala Vernon's Life," 191; "First Wars," 192; "Henry Sophona," 192; "Passages in the Life of an Individual," 194; lists Gondal character names, 195

Brontë, Charlotte: discovers Emily's manuscript "Gondal Poems," 11, 30–

General Index

Julius of Angora. *See* Brenzaida, Julius

Kingston, Eliza Jane, 36

Law, Sir Alfred, 18, 20
Livingston, Luther S., 36
Livingston, Mrs. Luther S. (Flora V.), 36
Lord Eldred W. *See* Gondal

Mott, Joan, 27, 168

Newby, Thomas Cautley, 35
Nicholls, A. B., 17, 19
Nussey, Ellen, 34

Parrysland, 13–15
Patchett, or Patchet, Miss, 34, 187, 191
"*Poems* by Currer, Ellis, and Acton Bell. "*See* Brontë, Anne; Brontë, Charlotte; Brontë, Emily

Rosina of Alcona. *See* Almeda, Augusta Geraldine

Shorter, Clement K., 16–17, 73, 129, 189, 194
Smith, Mrs. George Murray, 20
Stark Library (The University of Texas), 19

The Twelves, 12

Wellingtonsland, 13–14
Wise, T. J., 17
Wooden soldiers, 12, 13
Wooler, Miss, 12, 32, 33, 187, 191
Wuthering Heights, 11, 30, 35, 36, 37, 71, 73, 74, 93, 168, 183

Young Men's Magazine, The, 13
Young Men's Play. *See* Angria; Glasstown